CW00730408

THE TIMES

BRITISH
ROYAL
FASHION

TIMES BOOKS

Published by Times Books
An imprint of HarperCollins Publishers
Westerhill Road
Bishopbriggs
Glasgow G64 2QT

HarperCollins Publishers
Macken House
39/40 Mayor Street Upper
Dublin 1, D01 C9W8, Ireland

First edition 2023

ISBN 978-0-00-865108-4

10 9 8 7 6 5 4 3 2 1

A catalogue record for this book is available from the British Library.

Our thanks and acknowledgements go to Robin Ashton and Joanne Lovey at News Licensing and, in particular, at The Times, Ian Brunskill and, at HarperCollins, Harley Griffiths, Evangeline Sellers, James Hunter and Rachel Weaver.

Printed by GPS, Slovenia

If you would like to comment on any aspect of this book, please contact us at the above address or online.
e-mail: times.books@harpercollins.co.uk
www.timesbooks.co.uk

This book is produced from independently certified FSC™ paper
to ensure responsible forest management.

For more information visit: www.harpercollins.co.uk/green

THE TIMES

BRITISH ROYAL FASHION

FROM THE REGENCY ERA TO MODERN DAY

Foreword by Anna Murphy
Edited by Jane Eastoe

Norman Hartnell.

CONTENTS

FOREWORD

t's a photograph that all of us can call to mind, that long-ago paparazzi shot of a 19-year-old called Diana Spencer in a skirt that, little did she know, the sunlight of a September day in Pimlico would render see-through.

It wasn't a fashion moment in the truest sense. Hers were ordinary clothes, if somewhat SW1-ish clothes, and this was the kind of wardrobe malfunction to which us lesser mortals could all too easily relate (although our versions of similar were not, thank goodness, for global consumption).

At the same time it *was* a fashion moment. Because that young woman would, of course, go on to become Princess Diana upon her marriage the following year to the then Prince Charles. That outfit would be passed ad infinitum around the world, just as every ensuing ensemble would be for the rest of her life.

Clothes are never just clothes when you are royal. In the modern era of the paparazzi, an era that was accelerated by – that coalesced around – Diana herself, with tragic results, this became more than ever the case. On-duty was on-duty, as it had always been. But off-duty was now on-duty, too. You couldn't get it wrong, ever. Potential exposure – albeit not usually of quite such a literal variety as offered by that skirt – was around every corner.

Diana going to the gym was fair game, just as, a generation later, her sons coming out of Mahiki's nightclub would be. Who could have predicted that those sweatshirt and legging-shorts combos of hers would prove a prototype for the now ubiquitous athleisure approach to dressing, in which every day looks like a gym day, even if it isn't? That Diana's greatest fashion legacy is not all that fabulous suiting, nor her infamous so-called revenge dress, but the garb she wore to and from the Harbour Club, is perhaps the most surprising development in the history of royal fashion.

Five years after that game-changing photograph, in 1986, the late Princess Margaret gave an interview to the *Times* that gave a unique insight into what it means to be royal from a sartorial perspective (see page 150). "I can rarely dress for fun," noted the Princess, who was then in her fifties. "I have very few home clothes, mostly working clothes. My working clothes are like most people's best clothes." Among other things, the point of difference, the Them and Us, was clear.

Margaret had more to say. Diana, her nephew's then-wife, had recently "said all the things I was saying 25 years ago," she continued. "Clothes aren't her prime concern. They weren't mine. But the fashion writers persist in treating her, as they did me, as if we were just unreal figures straight out of *Dynasty*."

In this she was half right. Certainly, when you sign up to be Fashion Director of *The Times*, you also sign up, among other things, to be a royal commentator of sorts. The rest of her evaluation was a tad myopic, however. A dynasty is precisely what the royal family is. Moreover, it is a a dynasty that is sustained at least in part by that very irreality by which she claimed to be so bemused.

William Shakespeare famously wrote that "all the world's a stage". Costumes matter on a stage. They are part of what tells the audience who someone is; what role they have; what is to be expected of them. If the world truly is your stage, the whole world, as is the case for the royal family, then what you wear has yet more import. If our royals were to seem too "real", for which read too normal, too like us, then wouldn't that start to erode the very foundations of God-given otherness upon which the institution is built? Their clothes have some heavy-lifting to do.

This is no longer as straightforward as it used to be, however, which I would argue makes writing about royal fashion the most interesting it has ever been. Ours is an increasingly egalitarian world. The royal family is no longer just the de facto anomaly it was conceived to be: at its heart now lies a more potentially problematic incongruity, one that opens it up to criticism and might even, ultimately – as has happened elsewhere in Europe – invoke its ending.

While many of us still don't want our royals to be quite like us, we also know on another level that this is precisely what they are: as capable of marrying the wrong people or putting their foot in it or being less than perfect as we are – some might say, more so. And we worry about the cost of it all, of them.

Today's royals know they must at least try to square that circle, and that this has to be done in part via what they wear. They know that they must endeavour to make what is truthfully a contradiction in terms, appear not to be. How to be just different enough, just expensive enough? That's one of the challenges facing the current incumbents, in their dress as in everything else.

This is at its most extreme in the loftiest vestiary realms of ceremonial dress. In the run up to the coronation of Edward VIII in 1937, an event that never took place due to his abdication, *The Times* published an exhaustive account of what the peers in attendance should wear (see page 110). Barons were allowed two rows of black fur in the white fur that edged their crimson velvet cape, for example; Earls were allowed three, Dukes four. (Yes, really.) At King Charles III's coronation 87 years later, in contrast, peers weren't allowed to wear robes at all until a last-minute U-turn. Charles was doing his best to keep it real(ish) at the same time as conjuring the prerequisite pomp and circumstance. Tricky.

An early act by the young Queen Elizabeth II might have been a harbinger of a change, when she used ration coupons to purchase the fabric for her wedding dress just after the Second World War. (The government gave her 200 extra coupons. Quite how that covered the 10,000 seed pearls with which the ivory silk was embroidered is anybody's guess.) Yet from that point on she made no further pretence at being, or dressing like, an everywoman, with her Norman Hartnell and Hardy Amies couture.

In many ways the current line-up of royal women still play the game according to the rules devised by her, the woman who was Queen for seven decades. This is not least because they worked so well. The female royals tend to wear colour, albeit not as full-on as her rainbow brights. ("If I wore beige, nobody would know who I am," she once said.) They default to flatteringly sleek, tailored lines rather than the frothiness favoured by an earlier generation again, the late Queen Mother. And, when relevant, they will make a subtle nod to a host country or cause with the jewellery they wear, or their chosen palette, thus signalling that they have given care and attention to where they are and who they are meeting.

They use clothes to get themselves seen, to signal their status, but also to show their respect to others; to express a kind of deference.

As for when they are off-duty – which for as long as we can still see them is not, as discussed, truly off-duty – they are dressed like the countrywoman that Elizabeth once was, all horsey hues, and practicality-focused restraint, even if, for the Princess of Wales, this comes with added skinny jeans.

Kate has changed things up in another more important way, too. Queen Camilla may not, in line with her predecessor, shop the high street, yet our future queen does. It's notable too that while King Charles is, by contemporary standards, something of a fop, what with his bespoke double-breasted suits and his silk pocket squares, his sons dress like upper-class everymen. They look bland, not expensive.

Let's be honest, though; we don't really care about the men much these days. A lot has changed since the world followed the every sartorial move of earlier properly full-on fops such as Edwards VII and VIII. It's hard to get excited about the Princes of Wales's collection of polo shirts and entirely unexceptional suits. Kate, on the other hand, with her gold Jenny Packham cape dress on the other hand? That still rings our bell.

Back in the real world, would any other woman who got married in Alexander McQueen, whose aforementioned Packham number will have set her back several grand, honestly be wearing Zara? Hmmm. The semiotics are clear, though the rationale is perhaps more debatable. The princess may wear plenty of designer togs but she is still you, and she is still me.

Yet shouldn't a future queen, with a clothes shopping budget that we can only dream of, be repping more consistently the best that her country has to offer fashion-wise? And should she really be supporting the environmental disaster that is fast fashion? Therein lies the double bind of being a modern royal. You can't please all of the people all of the time. But you have to keep on trying.

Anna Murphy

INTRODUCTION

The British royals are probably the most photographed people on this planet. They are, and have always been, subject to the kind of scrutiny that would fell most of us. Watched, served and guarded night and day, this small group of individuals protects its image carefully.

Where once their own portraiture and official photography dictated how the public saw them, today they must negotiate a digital and online free-for-all.

For the most passionate monarchists, the family is still bathed in medieval mysticism, divine beings occupying an entirely separate social class, long to reign o'er us. For others, they have become popular performers in a never-ending live-stream soap opera. To their detractors, the royal family are an increasingly irrelevant anachronism, living a life of immense privilege thanks to an overgenerous allowance from the national purse.

From whatever standpoint, it is easy to see why the royals are never off duty. There is always the danger of a lurking unseen camera all too ready to record an image they would prefer no one saw. Anything unseemly threatens the position of the monarchy, and following the First World War and the collapse of the Russian, German, Austro-Hungarian and Ottoman empires, as well as the overturning of several smaller European monarchies, the British royals faced a very real threat.

To avoid a similar fate they made a conscious effort to remain popular and relevant, ranking up public appearances, walkabouts and tours, and supporting worthy causes. Withdrawing from public view, as Queen Victoria did, was no longer an option.

Thus for the royal family appearances are everything. Royal clothing is a form of armour, a tool of the trade that projects a regal and dignified front. They dress, by and large, quite unlike anyone else, but their influence is nevertheless, huge.

We are bombarded with their images and no other group, save Hollywood and music stars, receive such attention. This alone makes them hugely influential in sartorial terms. The compilers of the best-dressed lists must focus their critical gaze on the people we see the most of and the royals, familiar right across the world, regularly rank high.

In this book we examine how the British royal family, from the most senior to the lesser players, have managed to project a multifaceted personality to suit changing social mores, economic times and political diplomacy. We see how they utilise youth and glamour, a dash of sparkle, colour, audacious accessories, and symbolic costume and uniform, to preserve and maintain the royal image. Even at play, on the racecourse, the golf course, or the ski slopes, we study every sartorial detail.

Bertie, Prince of Wales, later Edward VII, became the world's first style icon. It may seem bizarre to us today that a portly, middle-aged chap should be pursued by what we now call paparazzi, anxious to record whatever stylistic change he had adopted. But Bertie, a distinctly snappy dresser, was a unique figure in a male-dominated society. He was heir to the largest empire the world had ever seen, was the father of a nation and was destined to be the most powerful man on Earth.

To contemporary eyes this is surprising, particularly as it is now the royal women that attract the most attention. The discomfort that Prince Charles felt when Princess Diana's dazzling allure outshone him was clear for all to see, but it marked a turning point. After centuries of male dominance women had firmly taken centre stage, not least because of the remarkable presence of Queen Elizabeth II, who had to adapt the traditional conventions of royal dress to suit the modern world.

As a young, beautiful and curvaceous woman, Queen Elizabeth could not hide behind the traditional camouflage of a pinstriped suit or uniform to reinforce the message that she was a national figurehead with power and status. Over a 70-year reign Her Majesty developed a remarkable wardrobe that helped maintain her authority and emphasise her position. The standards she set are the benchmark by which every other royal is measured.

The worldwide fascination with what is, after all, a group of only a few dozen individuals, is made more intense when a newcomer is recruited to 'The Firm'. Pity then the poor Diana Spencers, Catherine Middletons and Meghan Markles of this world who have to adapt and conform to a whole new dress code. Their clothes and personal style will be analysed and critiqued in acres of copy. Any fashion *faux pas* will be held up to public ridicule. Not so the men who marry into the royal posse. Has a single inch been written about the personal style of Jack Brooksbank or Timothy Laurence?

The coverage of royal events in *The Times* mirrors this development. It was once clearly regarded as bad manners to comment on royal dress, bar the briefest snippet. A Court report might detail the colour and style of dress of each and every lady in the royal presence, but of Their Majesties' outfits no mention was made. Nonetheless they were influencers. The Court followed the royal style lead and the trickle-down effect filtered through the ranks of society. Even a maid could trim her hat in the same style as the monarch.

In the post-1918 era, with more women entering the workplace, the newspaper gradually changed its approach. Royal dress became something its readers wanted to know about. *The Times* learnt that extensive royal coverage sold more papers and in turn pulled in more advertisers. In short, extensive royal fashion coverage made good economic sense and it started to snowball.

Profoundly aware that any wardrobe malfunction would cause a sensation – just look at the furore caused when a photographer focused on a tiny hole in King Charles's sock in 2023 – the royals were forced to dress to standards the rest of us cannot hope to achieve.

No one takes offence if we wear the same outfit twice. We do not have to think about flattering our hosts at events by wearing a particular colour or motif. We do not have to change our outfits four or five times daily for different functions or be unduly concerned when someone turns up in the same dress. We do not have to justify purchasing something that is made in another country instead of Britain. We have the liberating freedom to dress without any effort whatsoever should we choose so to do and, equally, we can spend whatever we like on clothes without public rebuke.

Theirs is not an enviable position. Certainly the royals can wear the kind of tailored or couture clothing that most of us can only dream of, but the planning and effort it takes to produce these quantities of clothing is phenomenal. In its essence this is a very specialist form of high-performance clothing that shields them and speaks for them.

We cannot get enough of it.

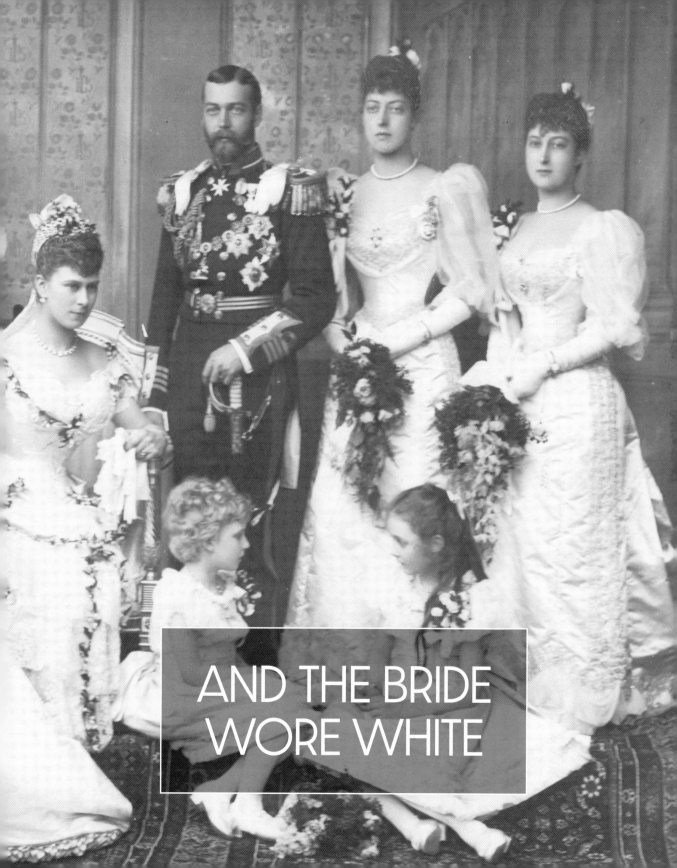

AND THE BRIDE
WORE WHITE

Lasting royal influence in fashion is seen most spectacularly in bridalwear. The sparkle, the glamour and the grandeur of "The Dress" has been inspirational for almost two centuries.

The older Queen Victoria in widow's weeds was no style setter, but as a 20-year-old bride she initiated the trend for white weddings. For her marriage on February 10, 1840, she avoided the silver or gold fabric favoured by her predecessors, selecting white as the best colour to complement her Honiton lace veil. She did this to support a struggling British lace industry and her ploy worked. Not only was Honiton lace popularised, but her British influence ensured many followed her diminutive lead. In the western world today reportedly four out of five brides still marry in white or some close shade.

Queen Victoria's wedding dress merited only a brief mention in *The Times* the following day: "Her Majesty came next, looking anxious and excited. She was paler even than usual. Her dress was a rich white satin, trimmed with orange flower blossoms. On her head she wore a wreath of the same blossoms, over which, but not so as to conceal her face, a beautiful veil of Honiton lace was thrown."

The first photograph of Victoria was not taken until 1844, so no precise visual image of her wearing this dress exists. A Franz Xaver Winterhalter portrait, presented to Prince Albert seven years after their marriage, is the most famous representation of her wedding attire.

In 1922 Princess Mary, the only daughter of George V and Queen Mary, and sister to future Kings Edward VIII and George VI, was the first to break from the tradition of formal courtly wedding dress. Elizabeth Bowes-Lyon followed suit when she married Prince Albert, Duke of York (the future George VI) the following year. Both were photographed in their shorter, dropped-waist styles, a difficult look to carry off but radically *à la mode*.

The marriage of the elegant Princess Marina of Greece and Denmark to the stylish Prince George, Duke of Kent, on November 29, 1934 attracted huge public interest, representing a growing national obsession with royal romance. Details of the bride's dress, by Edward Molyneux, including a sketch, were released in *The Times* in advance of the wedding, along with details of garments in her trousseau. The fact that she paid no import tax on her wedding dress caused a minor scandal.

In contrast, details of the wedding of the Duke of Windsor, the former Edward VIII, to twice-divorced Wallis Simpson on June 3, 1937, are scant. *The Sunday Times* reluctantly reported on May 30: "The Duke, it is understood, will wear morning dress; Mrs. Warfield will wear a long-skirted cocktail dress in blue crepe, a shade between pastel and hyacinth blue."

The cleric who performed the religious ceremony, without the authorisation of the Archbishop of Canterbury, merited more column inches in *The Times,* but we must recall that the paper's Editor Geoffrey Dawson was a key figure in turning public opinion against Edward VIII.

In the postwar era, wedding scrutiny increased significantly along with most aspects of the royals' lives. In a time of austerity and rationing *The Times* observed that the wedding of Princess Elizabeth to Lieutenant Philip Mountbatten in 1947 was "a tonic for the nation".

In July 1981, as Lady Diana Spencer's wedding to Prince Charles approached, *The Times* Fashion editor Suzy Menkes astutely observed it was Norman Hartnell, the designer of the wedding dresses for both Princesses Elizabeth and Margaret, who created the contemporary notion of the fairy-tale bride with his full-skirted designs and intricate beading.

Most modern royal brides have continued to live up to this romantic ideal, while the groom settles for one of any number of ceremonial uniforms. Attention at any royal wedding concentrates on "The Dress". An adoring public is eager for more style pointers for its own big day.

We proffer an account of the wedding dress prepared on this occasion for Her Royal Highness the Princess Charlotte

From our correspondent

May 3, 1816

The wedding dress, composed of magnificent silver lamé on net, over a rich silver thread slip, with a superb border of silver lamé; the embroidery at the bottom forming shells and bouquets; above the border an elegant fullness, tastefully displayed in festoons of silver lawn, and finished with a very brilliant rouleau of lamé. The body and sleeves to correspond, trimmed with beautiful point Brussels lace. The mantle of rich silver tissue, lined with white satin, trimmed round with a superb silver lamé border in shells, corresponding with the dress, and festooned in front with diamonds. Head dress, a wreath of rose-buds and leaves composed of brilliants.

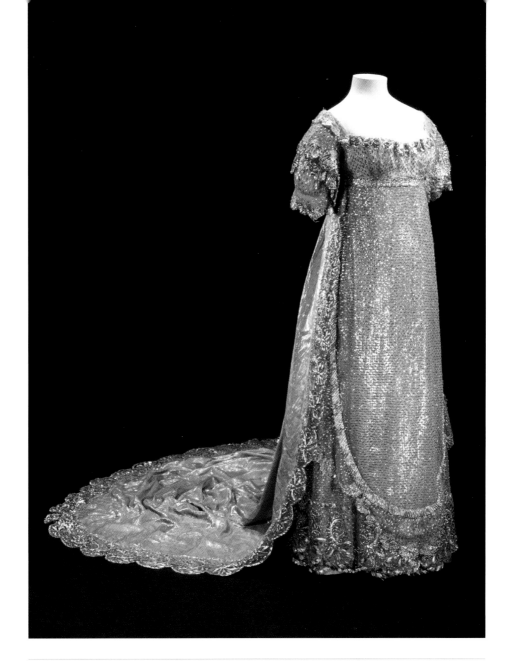

Princess Charlotte, the only child of George, Prince of Wales, later George IV, and Caroline of Brunswick married Prince Leopold of Saxe-Coburg-Saalfeld at Carlton House London on May 2, 1816. Her ensemble was designed by Mrs Triaud, a London dressmaker. It is currently part of the collection owned by Historic Royal Palaces but is now very fragile. Charlotte died in childbirth, just a year-and-a-half after her wedding, after being delivered of a stillborn son. Had she lived, she would have become Queen Charlotte. Instead, William Duke of Clarence (William IV) acceded the throne in 1830 upon the death of his brother.

Brides rush to follow Queen Victoria's lead

Left: The 20-year-old monarch, Queen Victoria, married Prince Albert of Saxe-Coburg-Gotha in The Chapel Royal, St James's Palace on February 10, 1840.

Right: The dress, which was made of cream silk satin had a pointed boned bodice and a full plain skirt gathered into the waist with pleats. The dressmaker's identity is uncertain, but it is thought to be Mary Bettans, who served the Queen for many years in this role. The lace was in part designed by Pre-Raphaelite artist William Dyce who was head of the new Government School of Design, which later became the Royal College of Art. The lace was woven in Honiton and Beer in Devon, and she wore this lace on her clothes for special occasions for the rest of her life. The dress was trimmed with orange blossom, made from wax, and she wore a wreath of the same on her head. She also wore a diamond necklace and earrings as well as a huge sapphire brooch given to her by Prince Albert. She was interred with her wedding veil over her face.

"...this was the happiest day of my life"

Mother-in-law-knows best

Princess Alexandra married Albert Edward, Prince of Wales, later Edward VII, in St George's Chapel, Windsor Castle. She was the first royal to be photographed in her wedding dress and what a dress it was. Unfortunately for Alix, as she was known, her mother-in-law was heavily involved in all decisions.

Her original wedding dress, made from Brussels lace, was deemed unsuitable by Queen Victoria. Firmly guided by Her Majesty, the new full-skirted court gown was made by Mrs James of Belgravia from white silk-satin woven in London's Spitalfields.

It had a low off-the-shoulder drawstring neckline trimmed with orange blossom and myrtle, puffs of tulle and the inevitable Honiton lace. This featured roses, shamrock and thistles and was made by Messrs. John Tucker & Co of Branscombe, near Sidmouth in Devon. The same lace design was used for the veil and the bridal handkerchief.

Always fond of jewellery, the bride wore a pearl necklace and earrings, a gift from her fiancé, an opal and diamond bracelet given to her by Queen Victoria, a diamond bracelet given by the ladies of Leeds, and a diamond and opal bracelet given by the ladies of Manchester.

The final effect was deemed very suitable for a future Queen. However it speaks volumes that the recently made Princess of Wales had her wedding dress altered in style after the great day.

Jane Eastoe

Princess Alexandra of Denmark (1844-1925) and Prince Albert Edward (1841-1910) on their wedding day, March 10, 1863.

Beloved youngest child married in Queen's veil

It took many years for Princess Beatrice to persuade her mother to allow her to get married; Queen Victoria could not do without her daughter, on whom she had leant heavily since the death of her husband. The monarch only gave permission on the condition that Beatrice and her husband, Prince Henry of Battenburg, continued to live with her. Beatrice wore a white satin dress trimmed with Honiton lace. She also wore her mother's veil, which was lent for the occasion. The bodice and skirt were decorated with garlands of orange blossom. On her head Princess Beatrice wore a diamond circlet decorated with diamond stars, a gift from her mother.

Jane Eastoe

Princess Beatrice on her wedding day, July 23, 1885.

The Princesses Mary

Left: Princess Mary, fondly known as May of Teck, was a great-grand child of George III. She was engaged to Prince Albert, Duke of Clarence and Avondale, the eldest son of Prince Edward and Princess Alexandra and second in line to the throne. However, Albert tragically died of influenza six weeks after their engagement. Growing close during the period of mourning, Albert's younger brother, Prince George, proposed to Mary, and she accepted his offer of marriage. Details of her first wedding dress, dubbed the "Lily of the Valley", had been released to the public shortly before Prince Albert's death and it was thought inappropriate for her to wear this dress for her wedding to Prince George. Arthur Silver of the Silver Studio was tasked with creating a second design. The white silk dress, shot with silver thread, was embroidered with roses, thistles and shamrock, trimmed with lover's knots and garlands of orange blossom, and flounced with Honiton lace. She wore orange blossom in her hair and a tiara on her head.

Above: The third child of George V and Queen Mary, Princess Mary was sister to two kings, Edward VIII – to whom she was particularly close –and George VI. At the age of 24 she married the 39-year-old Viscount Lascelles in Westminster Abbey on February 28, 1922. It was the first time the child of a monarch had been married at the site since 1290. Elizabeth Bowes-Lyon, future wife to her brother and later queen consort, was one of her bridesmaids. Princess Mary's wedding dress was made by Messrs. Reville Ltd. The dress was made using a cloth of silver that Princess Mary had purchased from India, decorated with crystal and pearl beads in a trellis scattered with roses. The train was made from ivory silk, woven in Braintree, Essex, and embroidered with emblems from the Empire: lotus flowers, maple leaves, wattle and ferns. On her head she wore a floral bridal wreath. Hers was the first royal marriage to be covered by fashion magazines.

Medieval echoes for a modern Princess

From our correspondent   *April 27, 1923*

And then we looked for the bride. The choir had collected in readiness to escort her. The great doors open once more, and we realise that in the battle of gloom and gleam, gleam has held the field. She comes on her father's arm. They stand waiting. An immense beadle, or other officer, garbed in a huge scarlet gown, comes softly up to hers. From his great hand dangles a little, white, very feminine object – a handkerchief bag, we judge it – which the bride has left in her carriage. She takes it, smiling her thanks. In her other hand she has a bouquet of white roses. She takes a step or two forward and lays it reverently on the Tomb of the Unknown Warrior, just there before the West Door. She must pass that tomb to reach the sacrarium and her waiting bridegroom. She will not pass it without having paid this silent tribute to the memory of all the tragedy, the heroism, the devotion which have made happiness possible for her and for the man of her choice.

At last the signal comes. At the distant east end of the church all is ready for her coming. The choir breaks into the hymn, "Lead us, Heavenly Father, lead us" and the bride's procession starts. Lord Strathmore's scarlet uniform makes the white and green of the bride look all the fresher and the sweeter. Behind her come her eight bridesmaids, they, too, white and green: first her two little nieces, Miss Elphinstone and Miss Bowes-Lyon, who bear her long veil; then Lady Mary Cambridge and Lady May Cambridge; and behind them, rising in order of height, Lady Mary Thyme and Miss Cator, Lady Katharine Hamilton and Miss Hardinge.

Prince Albert, Duke of York, proposed twice to Lady Elizabeth Bowes-Lyon and was turned down on both occasions, but his persistence paid off, for she accepted him on the third time of asking. The bride's dress was designed by Madame Handley-Seymour to complement a length of Flanders lace, a gift from the groom's mother, Queen Mary. This length formed two trains: one from the shoulder and one from the hips. The dress was made from ivory chiffon moiré and embellished with bands of silver lamé as well as a strip of antique lace, a Strathmore family heirloom. The design was said to be based on a frock created by the Parisian couturier Jeanne Lanvin. It was embroidered with silver thread, decorated with seed pearls and girdled with silver. Low on her head the new Duchess of York wore a chaplet of leaves with a few white York roses.

How Princess's chic fell foul of native customs

Secret papers reveal row over foreign royal's love of French fashion

By Richard Ford

May 26, 1998

It was the most glamorous society wedding of the year. George V's fourth son was marrying a Princess whose style had brought her the admiration of Paris.

But the pending arrival of Princess Marina of Greece provoked a different reaction in London. Secret government papers show that a Whitehall battle took place over the embarrassing question of whether her wedding presents, and a lavish trousseau from a French fashion house, should be exempt from Customs duties.

As Customs feared that it could lose considerable sums, the Treasury revived the age-old rivalry between French and English couture. The Permanent Secretary to the Treasury went so far as to consult the best-dressed women in London over the merits of Paris versus London couture.

The papers, released at the Public Record Office at Kew, show that, instead of purchasing tiered silk lingerie, coat and dresses from the Paris fashion house of Molyneux and other items at Madame Suzy's, the Treasury thought the princess should set an example and buy British.

She had spent £202 (about £12,000 at today's prices) on a trousseau that included three morning ensembles, five afternoon dresses, six evening gowns and two coats. A woman's coat cost an average of £3 at the time and a railman earned £286 a year.

The tale of the princess, Customs, and her penchant for couture clothes from Paris has remained secret since 1934, when she arrived in Britain to marry Prince George, later the Duke of Kent.

The papers do not disclose who made a request for an exemption, but two months before the Westminster Abbey wedding, a Treasury minute stated that, without it, duty should be charged on goods imported by the Princess, who was the younger daughter of Prince Nicholas of Greece and a first cousin of the Duke of Edinburgh. The Treasury produced a memorandum written by Gladstone in 1874 which stated that, apart from the Sovereign, the royal family were liable to duty on goods entering the country.

The memo stated that duty would be payable on goods

imported by the princess and on wedding presents sent to her and Prince George from abroad. "If Princess Marina receives valuable presents from abroad of jewellery, for example, the duty might come to a considerable sum," Sir Evelyn Murray, chairman of the Board of Customs and Excise, said.

But three days later, on October 12, the Treasury agreed to exempt the wedding presents from duty but not the trousseau or anything else. A memorandum by Donald Fergusson, principal private secretary to the Chancellor, said that to exempt the trousseau "might excite criticism in Parliament".

The issue of the trousseau – which, along with the wedding dress, was being made at the Paris premises of the English-born couturier Edward Molyneux – continued to exercise high-ranking Treasury officials.

Mr Fergusson wrote: "It is open to the princess to escape the duty, if she wishes, by buying all her trousseau in this country. But if the princess prefers to buy her trousseau from a country other than that in which she is married, she must herself

pay the appropriate import duty." There matters rested, with an agreement that, "as a foreigner of distinction", her luggage would not be opened on arrival. But she had to prepare a list of its contents to allow duty to be assessed.

But, six days before her arrival on November 21, 1934, it became known that the exemption had upset her future mother-in-law, the formidable Queen Mary, and her fiancé.

A note from Sir Warren Fisher, Permanent Secretary at the Treasury, said that Queen Mary and Prince George were said to be "very annoyed" about the concessions. Sir Warren wrote to Sir Clive Wigram, private secretary to George V, that the concession was extra-statutory and therefore "strictly illegal" and could be challenged by MPs.

He was damning about the princess's desire for a trousseau purchased in Paris when Britain was still in depression. "It would surely be a proper and graceful act on her part to avoid foreign-manufactured goods, particularly at a time when this country has peculiar difficulties, and example is therefore of the first importance," he wrote.

Sir Warren added: "I am not, of course, an authority on women's attire, but I am assured by some of the best-dressed women I know that there is today nothing that cannot be bought in London that does not compare favourably with clothes purchased elsewhere. Moreover, if it were the case that it is impossible to be well dressed except in French clothes, I am further told that there are in London branches of French firms." Edward Molyneux had premises in both London and Paris.

When the accounts were finally delivered after the wedding, they showed that the princess had spent a total of £179 on a trousseau at the Molyneux fashion house, including £109 on couture, £47 on lingerie and £15 on a coat trimmed with ocelot. A further £23 was spent on the trousseau at Madame Suzy's.

The duty paid on the trousseau was a total of £72 (about £4,000 at today's prices) and the duty waived on wedding presents to the couple totalled £475 (£28,000).

As the new Duke and Duchess of Kent went on honeymoon, Major Ulick Alexander, Comptroller of

WEDDING OF T.R.H. THE DUKE OF KENT & PRINCESS MARINA.

PRINCESS CATHERINE   LADY IRIS   PRINCESS EUGENIE   T.R.H. DUKE & DUCHESS Gd DUCHESS KYRA   PRINCESS IRENE   PRINCESS JULIANA
OF GREECE   MOUNTBATTEN   OF GREECE   of KENT.   OF RUSSIA   OF GREECE   OF HOLLAND
            LADY MARY CAMBRIDGE   PRINCESS ELIZABETH OF YORK

A cousin to the young Philip of Greece and Denmark, later Duke of Edinburgh, Princess Marina married Prince George, the fourth son of King George and Queen Mary and also her second cousin on November 29, 1934. There had been no royal wedding for 11 years, so this was a significant event. The public were riveted by this handsome young couple and theirs was the first wedding to be broadcast on the radio, the control room in Westminster Abbey was below The Tomb of the Unknown Warrior. Details of the dress were announced ahead of the wedding, designed by the Paris-based English designer Edward Molyneux, it was made of white and silver lamé brocade which was both fashionable and chic. The veil had been worn by Marina's mother, and it was secured by The Kent City of London Fringe Tiara, a wedding gift. The duke wore the ceremonial dress of the Royal Navy, his oldest brother Edward, Prince of Wales, was his best man and his niece, eight-year-old Princess Elizabeth (seated right), was one of the eight bridesmaids. Ernest Simpson and his wife Wallis were guests at the wedding.

their Household, wrote to Sir Evelyn apologising for causing so much trouble and delay over the issue. "But I feel sure you can appreciate the difficulties I have had to contend with," he said.

The duchess was widely acclaimed for her sense of style and for bringing continental chic to the royal family. She was regularly in the list of the world's best-dressed women. Yet, 12 years later, when the duchess was preparing to go on an official tour to the Far East, her staff applied for a purchase-tax concession on clothing bought for the trip. It was politely but firmly rejected.

The 'Primavera' Princess

In postwar Britain the marriage of Princess Elizabeth, daughter of King George VI and Queen Elizabeth and heir to the British throne, sent the public into a frenzy of anticipation.

The 21-year-old princess, who was marrying Lt. Phillip Mountbatten, was determined to keep details of her dress a secret – she did not want any copies being produced in advance of her big day.

Norman Hartnell was chosen to design the dress and he had just three months to make it. Elizabeth had saved up her postwar ration coupons, and the government gave her 200 extra. The dress was made from ivory duchesse satin and smothered in crystal beading and seed pearls which were imported from America. These were stopped at customs until the duty had been paid.

Inspired by the Botticelli painting *Primavera*, the dress was decorated with beaded wheat sheaves, orange blossom, lilac, jasmine and star flowers, which also featured on the veil. It had a sweetheart neckline, a fitted bodice and flared skirt, tight sleeves and a full court train of 15 feet (4.5m).

On her head she wore Queen Mary's Fringe Tiara. Her bouquet of white orchids went missing but was found in the porter's lodge where it had been placed to keep cool.

Prince Philip wore his naval uniform and the eight bridesmaids included Princess Margaret, the bride's younger sister.

Jane Eastoe

Princess Elizabeth on her wedding day, November 20, 1947.

Gossamer silk in wedding dress

From our special correspondent　　　　　　　　　　*May 7, 1960*

As Princess Margaret moved slowly and gracefully on the arm of the Duke of Edinburgh up the long stretch of vivid blue carpet in the Abbey, it seemed she moved in a soft white cloud, whiter and gentler by contrast with the fire of diamonds on the small dark head.

Rumour was only partly right on the subject of the wedding dress. True, it was exquisitely simple, of white silk organza with a rather high V-neck showing the gleam of a narrow diamond necklace at the throat. But the tight-fitting sleeves were full-length, and three layers of the gossamer silk on a stiffened tulle foundation billowed out from the Princess's tiny waist in 12 sharply widening gores extending at the back to a slight train. Adding apparent height, a narrow rouleau of the fabric marked the vertical line of each seam. According to a spokesman for Norman Hartnell, the designer, more than 30 yards of fabric were used for the top layer only of the dress, apart from the foundation.

A similar rouleau held the tulle veil that cascaded lightly down, floating over the skirt to just beyond the line of the train. It was held by the high diamond diadem, small in diameter and set straight on the bride's head.

White crepe court shoes designed by Edward Rayne, with a white satin facing and slender 2-inch heels, completed the outfit.

The eight little bridesmaids, led gallantly by Princess Anne, looked as delicate and pretty as can be in dresses that were exact copies of Princess Margaret's own first evening dress, one that was a favourite of her father, King George VI.

Also of silk organza, with short, puffed sleeves set into a deep yoke finished with a Peter Pan collar tied with a blue bow, they had panels of fine broderie anglaise slotted with pale blue ribbons, falling from a rather high waistline to the frilled hem of the ground-length skirt.

With these were worn white kid shoes, and headdresses of tiny white bows and flowers of white feathers, dusted lightly with diamante. These dresses were also designed by Norman Hartnell.

The notion of the groom not seeing the dress didn't quite work out when it came to Princess Margaret's wedding. Her fiancé, Antony Armstrong-Jones was very interested in design and not only was he present at her initial meeting with Norman Hartnell to discuss the dress, he even produced a sketch of what was required. He curbed Hartnell's decorative excesses and Ian Thomas, the designer's assistant, heard Hartnell later proclaim: "It'll be nothing more than a nightgown". In fact it was a triumph, though the six layers of organza in the skirt, which were bound at the hem with an organza rouleau, caused something of a heart-stopping moment the day before the wedding when it was discovered that some had begun to shrink. The rouleau had to be removed and the skirt redone, but everything was completed on time. On her head Princess Margaret wore the Poltimore Tiara, which she purchased for £5,500 (about £105,000 in today's prices). Short in stature she adored that it was tall and added to her height.

Romance in cascades of silk

By Suzy Menkes

July 30, 1981

The romantic ruffle that the Princess of Wales has made her fashion hallmark was the focal point of her fairytale-wedding dress. A gentle flounce of ivory taffeta, overlaid with a second tier of pearl-encrusted lace framed her sweet young face and long neck, which was entirely free of the state jewels that had been expected.

The impression given as she stepped from her glass coach, with a full skirt below a tiny waist and the shimmering train snaking behind her, was of freshness and romance.

The same summer magic was seen in the bridesmaids' dresses, particularly in the flounced and scalloped calf-length frocks of the younger girls. With their garlands and baskets of meadow flowers, they could have been plucked from a Victorian child's scrapbook.

The golden Mountbatten roses – the same yellow echoed in the bridesmaids' sashes and in their flowers – was a poignant reminder

Wedding Gown of The Lady Diana Spencer

Left: the Princess of Wales's wedding dress sketched by its designers, David and Elizabeth Emanuel. The body of the dress is made of ivory pure silk taffeta. The bodice has a frilled neckline with intricately embroidered lace panels at front and back. The full sleeves are gathered at the elbow above lace petticoats of ivory tulle and trimmed at waist and hem with embroidered lace. The sweeping train is trimmed and edged with sparkling lace. The dress and veil are hand-embroidered with tiny mother-of-pearl sequins and pearls. A tiny gold horseshoe studded with diamonds, crafted by Douglas Buchanan, was added for luck.

of the much-loved member of the royal family missing from this happy occasion.

The Princess of Wales's dress was a triumph both in its overall conception and in its tiniest detail. David and Elizabeth Emanuel, the designers, managed to give the right sense of theatre and drama to a gown which we first glimpsed under a froth of veiling and then saw with its 25-ft train splashed dramatically across the blood-red carpet in the cathedral aisle.

The confetti shower of hand-embroidered mother-of-pearl sequins that spangled both the tulle veil and the antique lace panels of the dress threatened to out-twinkle

the rather simple Spencer family tiara that sat above the Princess's famous fringe.

The creamy lace panels (a flounce of Carrickmacross lace presented to the Royal School of Needlework by Queen Mary) was dyed just a shade lighter than the ivory silk taffeta of the main dress, with its low neckline and central bow. This gave a pretty contrast of tone on the bodice and to the edge of the gathered sleeves, as the Princess laid her pale arms against her husband's naval uniform.

The bride's shoes barely peeped out from under the layers of ivory tulle of the puff ball skirt, but they were intricately detailed. Nearly 150 pearls and over 500

sequins decorated the heart-shaped central motif of those silk Cinderella slippers.

The delicacy of detail and of colour were the most surprising notes in an occasion when fashion is always fairly predictable.

The first copy of the wedding dress appeared in an Oxford Street shop window barely five hours after the ceremony (the Press Association reports). It was created by Ellis Bridals, a West End company, who set to work the minute they glimpsed Lady Diana leaving Clarence House. A polyester satin copy was sent to Debenhams department store by 4pm, where it now bears a £450 price tag.

Strong clean lines, minimal fussy details

By Lin Jenkins

July 15, 1994

The royal family turned out in force yesterday for the marriage of Lady Sarah Armstrong-Jones to Daniel Chatto in central London.

Lady Sarah, 30, wore a dress designed by Jasper Conran similar to those worn by her three bridesmaids, Lady Frances Armstrong-Jones, Zara Phillips, daughter of the Princess Royal, and Tara Noble Singh.

She arrived at St Stephen, Walbrook, in the Queen's Rolls-Royce with her father, the Earl of Snowdon. Her mother, Princess Margaret was also present, as was her brother, Viscount Linley, and his wife Serena. Thousands lined the streets to greet the couple, despite their insistence on a quiet and personal service. The bride, 30, and her husband David Chatto, 37, both artists and renowned for their unconventional ways, chose to embrace tradition despite their quirky choice of church. They achieved their ambition of having an essentially quiet and private wedding.

Although it was not strictly a royal wedding, hundreds lined the streets around the Wren masterpiece only a stone's throw from St Paul's. St Stephen Walbrook seats only 200; the service was taken by the Prebendary, Dr Chad Varah, who is 83.

Lady Sarah's parents, Princess Margaret and the Earl of Snowdon, who are divorced, both beamed. Their son Lord Linley, who last year chose St Margaret's, Westminster, for his high society wedding to Serena Stanhope, left with his new bride on his arm.

Lady Sarah and Mr Chatto, who have enjoyed a discreet relationship for seven years, chose seventeenth-century baroque music for the short service. They left the church to cheers and confetti from a crowd kept well away by a police cordon to attend a reception at Clarence House, the London home of the Queen Mother.

Lady Sarah in her Conran dress with her bridesmaids outside St Stephen, Walbrook. "Conran's design for Lady Sarah Armstrong-Jones was one of the best royal wedding dresses in the past 50 years," Lisa Armstrong wrote for *The Times* in 2011.

Camilla's style wins over the fashionistas

By Claudia Croft

April 10, 2005

Elegant and understated, Camilla, now Duchess of Cornwall, entered the Guildhall in Windsor wearing an oyster silk basket-weave coat over a chiffon oyster-coloured dress and a wide-brimmed hat adorned with feathers and lace.

Commentators praised the outfit for its simplicity. It was the first of several worn by the Duchess on her wedding day.

For the blessing in St George's Chapel, she opted for a floor-length, porcelain-blue silk coat dress embroidered with gold, changing back into the first dress later.

Elizabeth Emanuel, who designed the wedding dress worn by Diana, Princess of Wales, said of Camilla's choices: "She looked very chic, very elegant, perfect for the occasion."

The handmade wedding outfits were designed by Robinson Valentine, the dressmakers based in Kensington, west London. They took 11 weeks to complete. Anna Valentine, the designer, said: "We wanted a crisp, clean look with subtle detailing for the Guildhall. For St George's Chapel we felt the dress should have a sense of occasion while remembering it was a blessing rather than a wedding."

Philip Treacy designed both hats worn by Camilla Parker-Bowles on the day of her wedding to Prince Charles, first at Windsor Guildhall for the civil ceremony, followed by a blessing of the marriage at St George's Chapel, Windsor Castle. In a break from tradition Prince Charles wore a morning coat instead of a uniform, the traditional attire of royal grooms.

The new Duchess of Cambridge knows what works on her

By Lisa Armstrong

April 10, 2005

For months the pat response from the miserablists was "Who cares about the dress?" In the event, a couple of billion people seemed to have worked up more than a passing interest, not least because, in an uncharacteristically deft spot of news management, Buckingham Palace kept its provenance secret right up to the great reveal. By 10.50 am yesterday The Dress – the last mystery in the pageantry jigsaw – was all anyone was talking about.

The bookies closed the book on Thursday at evens. And lo, their faith was rewarded. The future queen did, indeed, wear a dress by Alexander McQueen, as the fashion industry hoped she would. Or, rather, by the late Alexander's protégée, Sarah Burton, who took over creative direction of the label last year – with much input, so we are told, from the bride.

Those who had muttered darkly that a "high-fashion" label with a reputation for headline-grabbing design statements and dark moods would produce a gimmicky disaster, or that Kate, who sometimes seemed to be the last fashion-neutral 29-year-old in the land, would be ambushed by the McQueen "vision", can rest at ease. There were no exaggerated shoulders, nothing aggressive about the corsetry. Instead, it looked to the reassuring example set by Grace Kelly when she married her prince in 1956.

Clever Kate and Sarah, as that was one of the few stand-out royal wedding dresses from the past century. Like Helen Rose, who designed Princess Grace's lace wedding dress, the catwalk-savvy Burton knows what works on a spectacular scale. And the new Duchess of Cambridge knows what works on her.

There were so many decisions. Hair up or down? The bride, along with her hairdresser, James Pryce, his boss Richard Ward and, apparently, a whole team of coiffeurs, opted for a compromise that looked relaxed but, crucially, sufficiently windproof not to conceal The Kiss.

Crown jewels or family ones? Another tactful choice, with the "halo" tiara, made by Cartier in 1936 and purchased by the future King George VI for his future Queen (later the Queen Mother) partnering the diamond earrings featuring oak leaves and acorns, inspired by the Middletons' new coat of arms – a gift to the bride from her parents.

The myrtle in her bouquet was cut from the bush at Osborne House planted in 1845 from a sprig given to Queen Victoria by her grandmother-in-law. Queen Elizabeth II also carried myrtle in her bouquet. The Firm's latest addition shows promising signs of being a diplomat in the making.

If the new Duke and Duchess of Cambridge's union is as successful as the one between Burton and the former Miss Middleton, the auguries for the House of Windsor are excellent. It's easy to be carried away on a wave of sentiment on these occasions, but from any angle, including stone-cold sobriety, the bride looked beautiful. I'm confident that we won't wake up on Monday

with dress hangover. This was a design that fulfilled every duty that England – and the global audience – expected. It was grand but not stiff, demure but alluring, traditional, with a neckline that nodded to the Windsors' Tudor antecedents and Westminster Abbey's history, yet its construction was modern and elegant. Or, to put it in non-fashion speak, it moved when the bride did, billowing gently in the breeze. Fears that Kate, besides wearing that ring, might channel the late Princess of Wales's meringue have been laid to rest.

As well as providing the main attraction, Burton was responsible for Pippa Middleton's graceful, satin-based crepe, cowl-fronted column dress, modelled on an off-the-peg McQueen design that Cameron Diaz wore in crimson to the Golden Globes last year.

Like her late employer, Burton is a perfectionist when it comes to cut and fabric. After the misfires of Diana's dress and that of the Countess of Wessex, British designers can hold their heads high again. These dresses fitted the slender Middleton sisters impeccably – and, despite

its scale, the bride's dress swamped neither her frame nor her personality.

In Burton, Kate picked a designer with a passion for British history. Burton will have been delighted to incorporate the hand-engineered lace made by the Royal School of Needlework. She will have been perfectly at ease slicing into the Chantilly lace that was used on the bodice, skirt and underskirt, and ensuring that each hand-cut lace flower was the same colour. The train – an impressive but not ostentatious 2m 70cm (8ft 10in) – was nicely judged, too, as were the romantic tulle veil, the 58 organza-covered buttons and the padded hips.

But let's cut to the chase: most of us will care less that the English lace was spun using the Carrickmacross technique than that it made Kate look slender, youthful and, as Prince Harry's quick recce of that V-neckline at the altar testifies, discreetly seductive. To create a dress that is museum worthy but also chic and compatible with its wearer's understated style is no small feat.

It was always going to matter what the bride wore. In choosing such a

prominent British fashion label instead of a safe Sloane dressmaker, the Duchess of Cambridge has sent out a powerful message about the calibre of British creativity at its best, and its wearability.

When Kate Middleton stepped on to the red carpet in front of the abbey, even staunch republicans and metropolitan cynics found themselves putting their resistance to wedding fever on hold.

The press release from Clarence House confirmed the details at 10.59am. By 11.10am the first "get the bride's look" email pinged in from the high street.

It wasn't like this with Charles and Diana. Fashion desks back then weren't deluged with emails from PRs informing them, in painstaking detail, which fascinator Lady Freddie was wearing. There were no fake tans, either (had the bride and her sister been St Tropezed, their teeth subtly lightened?). And the country probably wasn't speculating about how hot the maid of honour looked.

Meghan Markle's best kept secret in simple silk

Surprise choice of designer produced a masterpiece of understatement

By Jane McFarland   *May 19, 2018*

From the moment Harry and Meghan announced their engagement in November last year, there was huge speculation about what the bride would wear.

It has been the best-kept secret in fashion — reportedly only the bride, the designer and two royal household staff knew until 12.03pm when Ms Markle, as she still was, appeared from a Rolls-Royce at St George's Chapel in Windsor.

It was Birmingham-born designer Clare Waight Keller, the artistic director of French fashion house Givenchy, who scooped the gig of the year to help transform the actress into the Duchess of Sussex.

Rather than invite comparison by choosing the same designer, or a similar style, as her sister-in-law, the Duchess of Cambridge, or echoing Diana's puff-sleeved gown, the bride opted for a chic, elegant dress reflecting the pared-down aesthetic we've seen throughout her personal wardrobe.

Designer and bride met earlier this year and worked closely together on the design.

Made of exclusive double-bonded silk cady, the slim-cut dress was created with six placed seams. The demure boat neckline framed Meghan's shoulders, while the slim three-quarter-length sleeves add a note of refined modernity.

A 16ft-long veil, made from feather-light silk tulle with a trim of hand-embroidered flowers representing the flower of each Commonwealth country, finished the look.

Queen Mary's diamond bandeau tiara, on loan from the Queen, was the only embellishment.

The bride once said her ideal wedding dress was the bias-cut slip that Narciso Rodriguez designed for Carolyn Bessette Kennedy in 1996. Her elegant choice today combined notes of Britishness with an international appeal.

While Givenchy, founded in 1952, is a heritage French house, Keller is its first female artistic director and a stalwart of British fashion. Her choice of designer is an encouraging sign that Meghan is committed to her new role at the centre of British life.

Something old, something new for the sisters York

Left: Princess Eugenie married Jack Brooksbank at St George's Chapel, Windsor Castle on October 12, 2018. Her dress had a tight bodice and full sculptural skirt and was designed by Peter Pilotto. She opted for a low-cut back to deliberately reveal her scar from a scoliosis operation. She wore the Greville Emerald Kokoshnik Tiara.

Above: Princess Beatrice married Edoardo Mapelli Mossi at the Royal Chapel of All Saints at Royal Lodge Windsor on July 17, 2020. It was a below-the-radar wedding held secretly once Covid regulations permitted small gatherings. The media were informed the following day. Princess Beatrice broke all the rules by wearing a vintage dress belonging to her grandmother, Queen Elizabeth. The dress, which the Queen had worn to the film premiere of Lawrence of Arabia in the early 1960s, was slightly remodelled to fit, and organza sleeves were added by Stuart Parvin and Angela Kelly. Beatrice wore the Queen Mary Fringe Tiara, which the Queen lent to her.

TAILORING

Royal patronage helped establish the worldwide reputation of Savile Row as the source of the finest bespoke tailoring. Craftsmen in cloth had started to congregate in the short street in Mayfair by the early 1800s but it was not until the 1860s, when the teenage Bertie, Prince of Wales, began frequenting the salon of tailor Henry Poole that The Row stood above all other places in producing clothing to the level of perfection required by gentlemen.

Other tailors also received royal commissions as Victoria's heir could change up to six times a day and had an outfit for every occasion – from a banquet to a visit to his beloved horse races. Always looking to combine style with comfort to achieve practical elegance, he was a menswear innovator, who introduced or popularised, for example, the modern lounge suit, the classic dinner jacket and the unmistakable Norfolk shooting jacket.

The principles of fine bespoke tailoring, in which every item is cut individually and sewn together with a great deal of handwork, created an immaculate image even for a man with the short and portly stature of the future King Edward VII.

The masculine ideal of classic tailoring – broad manly shoulders tapering across a full chest to a slim waist, all carried on long and muscular legs – is inspired by, and best exemplified by, ceremonial military uniforms. All the male royals have served in the Armed Forces and rapid promotion plus honorary appointments in all three services meant regular updates of new uniforms.

George V was particularly happy in a uniform and the martial tradition was carried off with aplomb by his granddaughter Elizabeth and her daughter Anne, both of whom have always looked comfortable and imposing in their military and naval uniforms. Both also seem very at ease in tailored daywear.

From his late teens to the end of his days, Edward VIII, first as Prince of Wales then as Duke of Windsor, was another menswear fanatic who discussed clothes in depth in a 1960 memoir, *A Family Album*. As he admitted, "I have always tried to dress to my own individual taste."

When his London tailor, Frederick Scholte, declined to make his trousers to be worn with a belt rather than braces, Edward had his desired modern trousers produced by H. Harris, a New York tailor who had served an apprenticeship in London. Scholte made the matching jackets.

The prince was rivalled in the style stakes of the 1920s and 1930s by his younger brother, George, Duke of Kent, who developed a comfortable double-breasted jacket style with his tailor Anderson & Sheppard that became known simply as The Kent.

Although George VI is often viewed as a conservative figure, photographs of him with his older and younger brothers confirm he was always impeccably and appropriately dressed. Following that stylistic mantra in the modern era was the Duke of Edinburgh, whose tall, slim frame was always superbly covered in pin-sharp uniforms or faultless single-breasted suits. He discovered a look that suited him early, and he stuck to it.

Queen Elizabeth II embraced tailored daywear courtesy of Hardy Amies. A couturier based at 14 Savile Row, he was largely responsible for dressing Her Majesty in smart but feminine tailoring to emphasise her status in a world dominated by men.

Prince Charles took somewhat longer to find his way. In his early days as Prince of Wales he lacked the verve of his dashing predecessors but by his thirties he had developed a personal style – best characterised by double-breasted suits – that saw him regularly on the best-dressed lists.

Reflecting the fashion trends of their era, the younger male royals have never been seen as champions of tailoring. William and Harry wear an Army, Royal Navy, or Royal Air Force uniform well, but generally they prefer chinos and polo shirt to a suit.

Catherine, Princess of Wales, looks very comfortable in her trouser suits from brands like Reiss but it is hard to imagine a male royal settling on something off-the-peg instead of bespoke.

The Playboy Prince

King Edward VII was the playboy prince who had to wait 59 years to succeed his mother, Queen Victoria.

As a result, he spent a large part of his adult life in the enthusiastic pursuit of all manner of pleasures and pastimes – and he was always appropriately and superbly attired, often in outfits he had devised himself.

As Prince of Wales, Bertie – as Albert Edward was known to his family and intimates – was an enthusiastic innovator. Much to the distaste of his mother and father, Prince Albert, he surrounded himself with a fast set, tastemakers of the day who followed his lead in matters sartorial.

Aged 17, Bertie was awarded an allowance of £500 a year (about £50,000 in today's values) mainly to buy his own wardrobe, but his father despaired at his heir's obsession. "Unfortunately he takes no interest in anything but clothes, and again clothes. Even when out shooting, he is more concerned with his trousers than with the game," he wrote to a family friend.

Much leisure time was spent at the royal estate of Sandringham, Norfolk. The reforming Prince was always wishing to be elegant but comfortable and practical, so he decided he wanted to simplify the tailcoat he was expected to wear for evening dinner parties.

In 1860, still in his teens, Edward requested that Henry Poole, at the time his principal tailor on Savile Row, cut off the tails of his evening tailcoat to make a shorter jacket that was easier and less fussy to wear.

The result was the modern dinner jacket, also known as a smoking jacket after one of the Prince's favourite vices. In the US this new style of gentlemen's eveningwear became known as a tuxedo after it was adopted by members of a smart gentlemen's club in Tuxedo Park, New York.

More than 150 years on, Bertie's dinner jacket is the standard men's garment for black-tie dinners. For both formal and informal occasions alike, Edward VII was a global trend-setter for the modern gentleman.

Jane Eastoe

The Prince of Wales projects haughty arrogance in this surprisingly informal portrait by society photographer Alexander Bassano. Taken about 1875, it shows 34 year-old Edward in a conventional daytime outfit – frockcoat, waistcoat, wing collar shirt, silk tie and contrasting trousers. The jacket has silk edging and the trousers a pronounced side seam. The silk top hat is set at a confident tilt. Note his chunky rings.

Victorian Strictures and Structure

Left: This undated photograph of Princess Victoria (1840-1901), Queen Victoria and Prince Albert's eldest child, reveals the complex construction of Victorian daywear. Note that she is not swathed in masses of jewellery; for a princess the look is relatively plain. After a three-year engagement she married Prince Frederick, later Frederick II of Prussia, in 1858 at the age of just 17. Together they had eight children. She became Empress of Prussia, in March 1888, but only for 99 days; her son Wiliam II acceded to the throne on the death of his father in June 1888.

Right: Princess Alexandra looks crisp and svelte in a dark dress with white trim details.

Mary: upright and unchanging

Left: Seen after visiting The Newman Gallery in central London in 1911, the new queen looks elegant and restrained in her well-fitted skirt suit and a typically striking hat. Princes Edward and Albert wear the uniform of the Royal Naval College, Dartmouth.

Right: This photograph is believed to date from 1906, when Princess Mary was in her early 40s and had given birth to six children. Her waist size shows the power (or the tyranny) of the fine corsetry of the era. The future queen was 5ft 7in but her slim, long skirt and large hat give the impression she was taller.

Why Wallis won't wear Chanel

By Ernestine Carter

April 15, 1962

The Duchess of Windsor is surely one of the cleverest women in the world at dressing herself. For make no mistake, her ineffable smartness is not due only to an income which permits her to be dressed by the greatest designers. I have seen women who manage to look dowdy in clothes by Mainbocher and overdressed in suits by Hardy Amies.

Selection of the clothes which she knows from study, as well as instinct, are just the right ones for her is the secret.

In an interview with *Women's Wear Daily* on her arrival in New York she said: "I can't wear Chanel. Too much. A chain here, a ruffle there." And she is right. Small neat women like the Duchess do not take well to Chanel's casual look. For them is the sharply defined pared-away chic of Balenciaga or Dior.

The Duchess confessed that she had even made Saint Laurent remove the fringe from his famous suit. "I had to get rid of all that nonsense," she said crisply.

Left: Arriving from the USA at Southampton aboard the Queen Mary on November 5, 1947, the pair are in typically stylish – and complementary – calf-length coats. The Duchess's version, with the waist cinched with a belt, suits her petite build better than the slightly-too-big option her husband wears.

Above: Photographed here in the early 1940s the Duchess of Windsor's wardrobe is showing no signs of wartime fatigue, but then she kept herself famously thin, existing on just an egg a day if she gained as little as two ounces in weight. Her supremely classic style meant that she could continue to plunder her extensive wardrobe to maintain standards despite being unable to visit the French couturiers.

Fashion moment

By Colin McDowell

April 16, 2006

There are many ways of being a queen. You can dress down or up. Dowdy or magnificent. But what you can never risk is being fashionable.

Unlike film stars and politicians' wives, queens have a long shelf life – sometimes spanning centuries – so they must find a timeless, understated style that, while never quite being in fashion, will never go out.

A queen's mode of dress must never make the next generation laugh when they see her image. That's why no queen who takes her role seriously would ever do the same with fashion.

The Queen was lucky from before the start of her reign. Hardy Amies, whose fashion house this year celebrates its 60th anniversary, was brought in to supplement the clothes made for her by her mother's dressmaker, Norman Hartnell. Whereas Hartnell favoured heavy draping and statuesque evening gowns so stiff they could virtually stand by themselves, Amies wanted something lighter and more modern.

He knew he had to tread carefully. The Queen wasn't especially interested in fashion and saw her public-occasion clothes merely as working dress. She shared her mother's abhorrence of Wallis Simpson, who was condemned for being nothing more than a fashion plate.

She also knew it would be a mistake to allow the dignity of her position to be undermined by attempts to follow the latest trend. Her only slip was when she allowed Amies to put her in a short skirt at the height of the mini's fashionability.

The error was never repeated, which is why the Queen has the priceless asset that, whenever she is mentioned, the largely unchanging image worked out for her by Amies is instantly conjured up. All over the world, even in countries with their own much-loved royal families, "the Queen" is taken to refer exclusively to the woman who lives in Buckingham Palace.

Queen Elizabeth II steps out to inspect troops in Sierra Leone in 1961 in a striking white silk dress by Hardy Amies. It is cut with a tulip skirt and a slightly low waist.

Left: Hardy Amies famously decreed that blue was the Queen's great colour. Here, in her fiftieth year on a trip to Washington DC in July 1976, she wears a Hardy Amies tailored coat and matching hat teamed with white accessories. She is wearing the Duchess of Cambridge's Pendant Brooch, which originally belonged to Queen Mary's grandmother, Princess Augusta, Duchess of Cambridge, who was painted wearing it in 1877. Queen Elizabeth II inherited it in 1953.

Above: In April 1952 the new queen makes her first ceremonial inspection of Grenadier Guards at Windsor Castle. She is still dressed in black two months after the death of her father.

State of grace

Only when Diana transcended fashion did she achieve the highest feat of chic: what she wore didn't matter, she just looked wonderful.

By Sarah Mower   *September 6, 1997*

In the last couple of years, and particularly months of her life, Diana had reached her ultimate state of grace. Here was a woman so in control of the clothes she wore, the accessories she chose, the casual raked-back way she did her hair, that she had performed the highest feat of chic for herself: what she was wearing had actually ceased to matter. All you saw was her and all you noticed was that she looked fantastic.

In the last days, Diana's clothes didn't scream Versace, though they mostly were. So seriously was her work taken by then that she had made it irrelevant even to ask who manufactured those stretch chinos and poplin shirts. The often embarrassing royal hats were long gone. The heavy state ballgowns were liquidated for charity. She had virtually given up wearing jewellery.

What remained, however, wasn't a princess who had renounced fashion but someone who had finally got it into its proper place, so that nothing (not even a dodgy swimsuit or two) interfered with the vision of a woman looking fabulously, glowingly, as the French say, *bien dans sa peau*. Happy in her skin.

It was a joy to see her hit that high – a shining example of the current international standard of minimal, luxurious chic. A plain shift dress. No tights. No rollers. No hairspray. Very little make-up, just low-key status accessories – Gucci bag, Chanel sunglasses and pumps for day, and a version of a slip dress at night. Tiaras strictly in the vault.

Whether she was going somewhere important, on a date or just scampering from gym to car, Diana personified the casualisation that has been the story of fashion in the Nineties. Arguably, she had always looked her youngest, sexiest best in casual clothes. The

indelible images of the fashion-icon's easy, golden style of her last days – and what they seemed to imply about her state of mind and sense of self – is perhaps the only consolation we have.

It took a lot of time, mistakes and work to look effortless. It was not true that Diana was a world-class fashion leader. She was something much more human and compelling – a girl who started out with ordinary, uneducated fashion tastes, who rose to a personal best no one could have believed. It was watching that process – the 17-year serial of what she'd wear next and whether it would work – that made us obsessed with Diana's clothes.

That she didn't always get it right was part of the entertainment, but it also endeared her to us and gave her that all-important quality of being real.

Diana, then Princess of Wales, created quite the stir when she wore this Moschino houndstooth suit for the christening of Princess Eugenie in December 1990. Proving the point that the royals do wear the same item, she wears it again on a visit to Portsmouth in October 1992 to receive the Freedom of the City.

Above: Diana, Princess of Wales, looks extremely comfortable in her skin in a pink, double breasted, short sleeved Versace suit. It's smart, chic and suits her perfectly.

Right: At a celebration to mark the 50th anniversary of VE Day in 1995 Diana, Princess of Wales, wears a pale blue suit with collarless jacket, matching hat and white accessories. Note the lack of hosiery, as she broke free of royal restrictions.

Objects of desire from the House of Windsor

By Alan Hamilton

February 9, 1998

They were arguably the most stylish couple of the century and were avid hoarders of everything they ever owned – especially their clothes. When the personal possessions of the Duke and Duchess of Windsor go under the hammer in New York later this month, it will take nine days to dispose of 44,000 items in the largest auction of royal memorabilia.

For a man who constantly pleaded poverty the duke had a remarkably extensive wardrobe, including 15 evening suits, 55 lounge suits and a kilt for every day of the week. As an arbiter of fashion, he popularised Fair Isle sweaters, plus-fours, tweed caps and the Windsor knot, which he considered the most elegant finish to a necktie.

The duchess once told a friend: "I'm nothing to look at, so all I can do is dress better than anyone else." She had a collection of shoes to rival that of Imelda Marcos, in quality if not in number, and every item of her silk underwear was monogrammed. Deprived of the title Royal Highness by George VI, Wallis did everything in her power to convince herself and the world that she was a Somebody.

Slopping about was not a thing that the Windsors did. Even when relaxing at weekends at their country retreat outside Paris, the duchess insisted on wearing kilts by Dior. Both were fastidious to the point of obsession, the duke wearing his wardrobe in strict rotation to prevent any item wearing out before another.

The result is that not only their wardrobes, but virtually every last possession of their lives together, survived in mint condition in their home in the Bois de Boulogne after the death of the duke in 1972 and that of the duchess in 1986. Now the collection is to be broken up. Sotheby's estimate its worth at about £5 million; others expect the auction to realise nearer £40 million.

The Duchess of Windsor, a true arbiter of style, wears the most exquisite piece of sharp tailoring, a perfect foil for her famous flamingo brooch. This photograph from August 1940 shows the couple en route for the Bahamas, where the Duke of Windsor was to become Governor.

But you can never tell with the Windsors. Their life was so unreal, so extraordinary, so perceived as a romance more touching than anything dreamt up by Hollywood, that virtually nothing in the auction, is likely to go for a song.

Someone will doubtless pay well over the £300 estimate for the Duchess's mink garters, if only because it's the devil's own job to find mink garters these days.

Above: As well as a slight build – Wallis was 5ft 2in, her husband 5ft 6in – the pair shared a love of bold fabrics and striking pattern mixing. Here their lapels mirror each other too. On September 13, 1939, 10 days after Britain had declared war on Germany, the couple were photographed at the East Sussex home of Edward "Fruity" Metcalfe, the Duke's equerry and best man at their wedding.

Heir to a dapper sense of dress

The Prince doesn't need to watch trends — he has inherited a regal sense of style

By Kate Reardon

October 31, 1998

Prince Charles dresses like an old-fashioned, rather sexy rogue. All those double-breasted suits and that ring twiddling make you expect a smooth "Oh, hel-lo" in the manner of Terry-Thomas. There is a bounderish smoothness about him that is so understated it could easily be missed. If we didn't know so much about him, he could be confused with the elegant cad who thwarts Bertie Wooster in affairs of the heart.

The earnest expression, matched with the hand casually half in the pocket, is far more the rakish old bachelor than the repressed ageing loony that we are told about in the papers. Could it be that while Diana, Princess of Wales, became famous for talking to the people through her clothes, Charles had been at it all along?

In a family not noted for making the best of themselves, Prince Charles is fortunate in inheriting the elusive Duke of Windsor fashion gene. Edward VIII was one of the most stylish men ever to have graced the planet, and the absolute trend-setter of his day. To many, the Windsor knot is still considered unbeatable. They also share a devilish love life, a fondness for flash friends and a love of sport. Edward VIII looked good playing golf in rakish plus-fours, whereas Prince Charles's sport of choice, polo, has the obvious advantage of white breeches. Some say there is little sexier than a man on a horse, and for all those tabloid pictures of him falling on his face, there are thousands of him looking fit and attractive.

Always impeccably turned out, he dresses as you would expect a member of the Royal Family to. But other members of the family never quite achieve the look of effortless perfection that Prince Charles has made his own. With never so much as a shoelace going off-message, his look would be fairly worrying in friends or acquaintances. But Prince Charles carries it off with such casual ease that there is never the worry that Camilla has had to fight him for mirror space.

The perfection that we can count on is vital to his appeal and so, when we see him looking less than polished, it is a little disturbing. A photograph of him in a stiff breeze with the royal hair standing on end may be amusing but it is uncharacteristic.

There is nothing cosy about the Prince of Wales's style. Very few daddies dress like him. No avuncular knitwear, no middle-aged disregard for the crispness of the shirt. This is a man who clearly takes an interest in personal hygiene, whether GQ says it's in fashion or not. The supreme confidence of his personal image is attractive. Masterful, even.

In true Terry-Thomas, posh-cad style, the Prince of Wales is prone to wearing institutional ties – the male equivalent of Chanel buttons. In Prince Charles's case he is paying a compliment to his hosts or a regiment. Although Princes William and Harry have been spotted wearing Ralph Lauren and Nike logos, this is the closest anyone will get to product placement on the heir to the throne.

It takes a confident man to wear a skirt at the best of times, but Prince Charles has a way with kilts. A lifetime of holidays in Scotland have taught him how to appear relaxed in a kilt. This is the closest to dressing down he gets. Not many men would bypass jeans and reach for a skirt when they want to let their hair down.

The time he fails to please is when he tries too hard. The English have a revulsion for being seen to try at all so, when it is not only obvious, but clumsy, all respect is lost. Those unwise, impulsive moments, usually on foreign

tours, when he poses with too many local accessories, he looks awkward and uncomfortable.

Luckily, these scenes are infrequent. Resolutely old-fashioned, the Prince has found a look that suits him and he is sticking to it. Like many women, whose life's work it is to shop for clothes, he has realised that there is little point chasing trends. Whether you think it's stuffy or not, there is dignity in the way he dresses. Prince Charles, like the Queen, looks exactly the way we

expect him to, and that is his appeal.

For four decades from the mid-1980s the then Prince of Wales found a look he liked in double-breasted suits. While it would not be everyone's first choice as an outfit for a walk through a wildflower meadow, seen here Charles looks relaxed in it. The suit certainly would fit better than this "moving" photo suggests.

Queen mourns Amies who defined her style

By Alan Hamilton

March 6, 2003

Sir Hardy Amies, the Queen's former dressmaker, who understood better than anyone the yawning gulf between sexy and chic, died yesterday at his Cotswold home at the age of 93.

Born the son of a north London seamstress, Sir Hardy rose to clothe the Queen for nearly half a century, and some of his creations are regarded as so enduring that they are on permanent exhibition in Kensington Palace.

Buckingham Palace said last night that the Queen was very sad to hear of Sir Hardy's death. "He contributed to her wardrobe over many years and she is, of course, saddened that he has died."

The master of the elegant cut largely retired from his royal commission when he reached 80, but took an active interest in his business until recently.

His association with royalty began in 1951, when the then Princess Elizabeth, who boasted an outstanding figure and a 23-inch waist, asked him to design a set of day clothes for an official visit to Canada. He was appointed the Queen's dressmaker in 1955 and perfectly understood the needs of his client, who has always emphasised to her couturiers that she is not a fashion model.

Rivals frequently regarded Amies's creations as dowdy, but the wearer liked them; one of her favourites was a white chiffon evening dress with a beaded Californian poppy motif, which she wore in Hollywood to a dinner with President Reagan.

"I don't think she feels chic clothes are friendly," Sir Hardy once said:

"The Queen's attitude is that she must always dress for the occasion, usually for a large mob of middle-class people towards whom she wishes to seem friendly. There's always something cold and cruel about chic clothes, which she wants to avoid."

Sir Hardy would counter criticism of his royal style by telling his detractors: "I dressed her for her job as Queen of England."

Sir Paul Smith, a fellow designer, said last night: "He made clothes that suited her status, her stature and her physique; he did a brilliant job for her." Sir Paul described Sir Hardy as one of the old school designers, a man who had a real knowledge of his trade. "In his early days he was very fashionable and among the few couturiers in Britain at a time when it was dominated by the French."

Alexandra Shulman, Editor of *British Vogue,* said Sir Hardy had been one of her heroes. "He became an international name decades before fashion was the global business it is now." International or not, the last thing Sir Hardy would have considered would have been to try to make the Queen look sexy. "Anything blatantly sexy can never be chic; overexposure of the body is not chic," he once said.

Sir Hardy's *bête noire* was the strapless dress, as it inevitably created the impression that the wearer was not completely relaxed. He explained: "I hate strapless bodices, because any man looking at one thinks, 'How the hell does she keep the thing up?' Nobody has ever been elegant in a strapless dress, because it implies that you're making your bust work for you."

Queen Elizabeth looked exceptional throughout her Royal Tour of India in 1961. Here, at a garden party in Delhi, she wears an exquisitely tailored silk coat and matching dress in silver grey, teamed with a divine matching hat, which must have taken some chutzpah to wear but she carried it off with style. The accessories are all white and she wears pearls and a diamond brooch.

Philip: Dapper across the decades

There was extraordinary consistency in the public persona of Prince Philip, who retained his slim, athletic figure and his preference for conventional single-breasted tailored jackets throughout his adult life. In August 1947 (**right**) his sports jacket was in a heavy Donegal-type tweed, while his shirt had long collars. In 1989 (**left**) for the stone-laying ceremony at Queen's College school in Barbados he prefers a modern lightweight cloth and a classic spread shirt collar. The similarity in practical simplicity is unmistakeable.

New era icon

Left: The Duchess of Cambridge seen here in London, October 2015, has worn this grey pleated dress with black daisy applique by designer Orla Kiely a number of times.

Right: At a St Patrick's Day Parade in Aldershot, 2014, the Duchess of Cambridge in a dark peacock blue coat from High Street retailer Hobbs with a dark green hat, a gold shamrock brooch, and a bunch of bright green shamrock at her lapel.

The Duchess of Cambridge wears a belted cream suit by the label Self-Portrait paired with nude suede shoes, a nude clutch bag and simple pearl earrings and necklace.

The Duchess of Cambridge wears a beautifully cut pale blue suit by Catherine Walker & Co on a trip to Netherlands in October 2017. Walker was a favourite of Diana. It is an exercise in disciplined and sophisticated design.

POWER
AND GLORY

Some elements of the royal wardrobe may inspire fashion copyists, but state and ceremonial dress remains an exclusive category. Chivalric costumes, little changed in design since the Middle Ages, reinforce the elevated and mystical status of the monarch's family. As *The Times* observed of Edward VII's coronation on August 11, 1902: "Here is the majesty of purple, the dress of kings; there the purity of ermine; here the pomp of scarlet, that colour which the blind in their attempt at realisation have likened to the sound of a trumpet ..."

In 2023, for the first time in 70 years, a coronation at Westminster Abbey showcased the most precious and powerful pieces of the royal wardrobe. The crimson velvet Robe of State worn by King Charles into the abbey. The gold silk *Supertunica* donned after his anointing. The newly-made purple satin coronation tunic, trimmed with gold artillery lace. For the departure from the abbey, the Robe of Estate, weighing a whopping 15lb, was a purple silk velvet robe trimmed with ermine and embroidered with sheaves of wheat to represent peace and purity. These unique garments are heavy with symbolism as well as with fabric and gold thread.

On June 28, 1838, Queen Victoria wore two outfits: a simple white satin gown with gold embroidery on the chest and a red robe for the start of the service, later replaced by a simple white satin frock. Her gold lamé *Supertunica* featured "gold thread on yellow warp brocaded in polychrome silk in a scrolling design incorporating Tudor roses, thistles and shamrocks, within scrolling design of stylised palm leaves".

Queen Elizabeth II asked Norman Hartnell, who had created her wedding dress, to follow the same line for her white satin coronation gown. The design selected from the eight ideas he offered utilised emblems of the home nations: the Tudor rose, the shamrock, the thistle and the daffodil. When Hartnell learnt the Welsh emblem was the leek, and not the daffodil, the embroidery was amended.

The Queen requested that emblems of her dominions should be included, so Canada's maple leaf, New Zealand's fern, the acacia from Australia, and the lotus from India. The emblems were embroidered in pale silk and highlighted with pearls, crystals and opals to create an iridescent sheen. Unknown to his client, Hartnell added a small detail of his own on the left side of the skirt – an embroidered four-leafed shamrock for luck.

The gown was technically difficult to make. The stiff, bejewelled and weighty skirt would not move correctly, so it was lined with cream taffeta and reinforced with three layers of horsehair crinoline to give a dignified gentle movement. At the final fitting Her Majesty described the result as "glorious".

Hartnell's design was deemed to be a masterpiece. In his book, *The Strenuous Years,* Cecil Beaton described the impact the Queen had at her coronation: "The cheeks are sugar-pink: her hair tightly curled around the Victorian diadem of precious stones straight on her brow. Her pink hands are folded meekly on the elaborate grandeur of her encrusted skirt; she is still a young girl with a demeanour of simplicity and humility. Perhaps her mother has taught her never to use a superfluous gesture. As she walks she allows her heavy skirt to swing backwards and forwards in a beautiful rhythmic effect. This girlish figure has enormous dignity; she belongs in this scene of almost Byzantine magnificence."

Beneath their flowing robes royal ladies traditionally wear white dresses to symbolise the purity and divinity of the monarchy. Decorative embroidery often features symbols of the four nations of the United Kingdom; but a couple of Jack Russell dogs were included with flowers and insects on Queen Camilla's dress, designed by Bruce Oldfield in 2023.

At the royal coronation of their most excellent Majesties King William the Fourth and Queen Adelaide

From our correspondent

September 9, 1831

At a quarter after 7 o'clock a body of the Foot Guards proceeded to line the road from the end of Parliament-street to the western door of the Abbey, where they were strengthened by two squadrons of Life Guards. Between 8 and 9 o'clock, several of His Majesty's Ministers arrived. They were all suffered to pass sub silentio (their persons, we presume, not being known to the million) except Lord Chancellor Brougham, who was immediately recognized, and was loudly cheered. At a little before 10 o'clock, a discharge of artillery announced that their Majesties had left St. James's Palace; and at a quarter before 11 o'clock, the head of the splendid cortege made its appearance.

The cavalcade proceeded amidst the most profound silence, until the carriage containing the Duke of Sussex appeared. The spectators then became actors, and loudly cheered his Royal Highness. Neither were they silent when the Duke of Cumberland was driven by. They gave his Royal Highness ample reason to say, "Populus me sibilat," both on his entrance and his exit. At length the state-coach approached the Abbey, amidst one

simultaneous burst of honest feeling – the best, the most grateful, tribute that a liberal and high-minded Monarch can receive. This was no common-place compliment which folly always offers at the shrine of exalted rank – it was the grateful meed which a generous-hearted people will always pay to a patriot King.

At this time the Royal carriage was stopped, in consequence of some slight confusion in the arrangement of the procession, for a few seconds. The acclamations were continued with the utmost fervour –

" – All tongues cried 'God save thee, William!'

"You would have thought the very windows spake,

"So many greedy looks of young and old

"Through casements darted their desiring eyes

"Upon his visage!"

Their Majesties appeared to feel very sensibly these manifestations of kindly regard, and bowed repeatedly. A few minutes before 11 o'clock, their Majesties entered the Abbey, and at a quarter before one the discharge of a rocket from the Abbey, followed by a salvo of artillery, announced to the metropolis that William and Adelaide were crowned.

Queen Adelaide in her coronation robes.

Left: At the age of 40 Queen Victoria was painted by Franz Xaver Winterhalter. This 1859 portrait shows her in sumptuous robes, wearing the Diamond Diadem, with the Imperial State Crown near to hand to project the image of regal power.

Above: 31 years later the 71-year-old Queen Victoria wears the same jewels for a portrait, painted by Heinrich von Angeli in 1890, though she has swopped the Diamond Diadem for her lightweight diamond crown.

Edward, then Prince of Wales, served very briefly in the Grenadier Guards in 1861 but a military career was deemed too dangerous for the heir to the throne. Among his honorary appointments, he was colonel of the 10th (The Prince of Wales's Own) Royal Hussars. When Edward acceded to the throne in 1901, he became colonel-in-chief of the fashionable regiment, which was nicknamed The Shiny Tenth because of its splendid dress uniform. This included a unique pouch-belt decorated with crossed metalwork worn across the chest. The uniform was dark blue with yellow braiding (known as lace) on the jacket, yellow stripes on their riding breeches, and a red bag and a white plume on the fur headdress, which is called a busby. Six rows of intricate frogging of differing widths promoted the masculine ideal of broad shoulders narrowing across a full chest to a narrow waist.

Queen Alexandra's abundance of jewellery is overshadowed by the Koh-i-Noor diamond set into her platinum coronation crown of August 9, 1902. The somewhat squat crown resembled European royal crowns in style. The Koh-i-Noor diamond is one of the largest diamonds in the world. Its origins are clouded in history, but it was "given" to Queen Victoria after the British East India Company annexation of the Punjab in 1849. Queen Victoria wore it in a brooch and a circlet, but she was not comfortable with the manner of its acquisition and said she did not enjoy wearing it.

The coronation robe of 1911

From our correspondent *November 30, 1910*

There is reason to believe that according to present intentions the King will wear at his coronation the imperial mantle or pall which was worn by King Edward on the occasion of his coronation in 1902.

This mantle resembles a cope and just fits on the shoulders, being fastened in front by a morse or clasp. It is made of cloth of gold woven from plate-gold threads worked upon silk. It was desired to obtain for the cloth of gold a peculiar shimmering appearance, so that in any light and from any point of view the cloth should glitter and sparkle with splendid effect.

A very great number of specimens of cloth were made, submitted and rejected before the one finally adopted was approved. Upon the cloth of gold is embroidered a design of laurel leaves forming a background rather subservient to the general adornment of the robe, which consists of emblems embroidered in various colours. This background is produced by fine stitches of the various silks used in the emblems, and these stitches again are covered over with silver and gold threads, the whole being drawn together with an outline of fine gold.

The background was introduced because the cloth of gold alone would have been too monotonous in its splendour, and also because the emblems could not be embroidered upon the surface with satisfactory effect without the provision of some subordinate scheme of decoration.

The emblems are encircled by the laurel leaves (which form wreaths or chaplets), and consist of the Imperial Crown, the Imperial Eagle, the Rose, Shamrock, and Thistle, and the Lotus Flower, the emblem of India. The Eagles are embroidered in silver, the Lotus Flower in white, the Rose, Shamrock, and Thistle in their natural colours. These emblems are repeated over the whole surface of the robe, and, with the laurel leaf ornamentation, add greatly to its richness and magnificence.

The mantle was embroidered at the Royal School of Art Needlework at south Kensington, of which Princess Christian of Schleswig-Holstein is president. All the materials used are of British manufacture. The cloth of gold was ordered by the Royal School from the Spitalfields Association, the actual makers being Messrs Warner, of Braintree, Essex.

King George V wore three robes during his coronation, beginning with the Royal Crimson Robe of State. The Golden Imperial Mantle is described by *The Times* above, but in this official photograph the King wears the final item: the Royal Robe of Purple Velvet – or the Robe of Estate. His cape was made of miniver pure (white fur from the winter coat of the Northern red squirrel) decorated with six rows of the black tails of ermine.

The Queen's gown and robe

The gown which the Queen will wear at the coronation, and which she will also wear at the durbar, is a princess dress made of deep ivory *duchesse* satin. It is richly embroidered in gold, eight or ten different kinds of gold thread having been employed for the purpose of bringing out the light and dark shades in the emblems introduced into the design. These emblems are the rose, shamrock, and thistle; the Star of India and the lotus lily. The last of these emblems is conspicuous in the embroidery round the skirt, where it appears to be floating on the surface of the water – an ingenious and beautiful effect introduced to represent the seas of Empire.

The gown is edged all-round the skirt with oak leaves and acorns. The dress has a train of considerable length, so made that it may be worn with the coronation robe. The embroidery extends over the whole of the front and back of the dress. In front, the Tudor rose, the shamrock, and the thistle, on separate stems are carried from the bottom of the skirt to the top of the bodice. In the centre of the bodice is the Tudor rose, supported by thistles, one on either side. The inner lace of the tucker is of Inishmacsaint lace, over which

is hand-made gold lace. The bodice is edged all round with a small shamrock. Hand-made gold lace and Irish lace are also used on the sleeves, which are short, ending just above the elbow and leaving the arms bare. The sleeves are caught together with two large thistles. The satin of the dress was made in England by Messrs. Warner, of Braintree, Essex. The dress and its embroideries were designed by Messrs Revillo and Rossiter Ltd, and the embroidery was made by Princess Louise's School of Needlework (the Ladies' Work Society) in Sloane Street.

The queen's robe, which is to be worn over the dress just described, was made by Messrs. Wilkinson and Son, of Maddox Street. The whole length of the robe from the shoulders to the extreme end of the train is six yards, and its width one yard and a half. It is made of royal purple velvet of English manufacture, woven at Sudbury by Messrs. Warner. In appearance it is extremely rich and regal. It is lined all through with the royal ermine, and a deep piece of the ermine is turned over the upper edge, making an effective contrast with the royal purple. On the part of the robe nearest to the shoulders are embroidered

in gold the rose, shamrock, and thistle. The lower part of the train is covered with an elaborate design, also worked in gold, in which the same emblems are introduced. In the middle of the design is the queen's monogram surrounded by the rose, shamrock, and thistle, all in gold. A beautiful effect is obtained by the introduction into the thistle heads of metal thread woven into the gold, which gives something of the appearance of the natural colour. The border of the robe is of oak leaves and acorns, and here the rose, shamrock, and thistle, worked into medallions, are again introduced.

A cape of royal ermine completes this robe, which is attached to the dress at the shoulders by gold cords and tassels. The robe, in addition to being of great length, is very heavy, and will therefore be borne by train-bearers – three on either side. The queen's shoes have been made of white kid and embroidered in the same way as the dress.

Her Majesty's fan, which is presented to her by the Fan-makers' Company, is made in England of exquisite lace from a design by Mr Woolliscroft Rhead, a member of the Company.

Previous page: Eight or ten types of gold thread were used to create the intricate design on the gown Queen Mary wore at the coronation in 1911.

Left: In a hand-tinted photograph, Queen Mary is seen wearing Order of the Garter robes and insignia and a stiffly-beaded dress with the appearance of chain mail. She wears her trademark high neck and strings of pearls.

Right: In this portrait of Queen Mary, by William Llewelyn circa 1914, she again displays the robe of the Order of the Garter and the insignia, but leaves off the ceremonial chain, preferring instead to pile on her famous jewellery.

Chivalric echoes of 1348

H.R.H. THE PRINCE OF WALES, K.G.

COPYRIGHT PHOTO BY
D. KNIGHTS WHITTOME,
SUTTON & EPSOM

The coronation of King George V and Queen Mary took place at Westminster Abbey on June 22, 1911, the day before the 18th birthday of their eldest son David. In the run-up to the event George's heir was created Prince of Wales at a ceremony at Caernarfon Castle and at St George's Chapel, Windsor. He was invested with the Most Noble Order of the Garter. He wore these Garter robes at Westminster Abbey where he paid homage to his father as part of the coronation service. Edward III founded this order of chivalry, the highest order of knighthood in the British honours system, in 1348. The ceremonial vestments include a mantle or robe in dark blue velvet lined with white taffeta. Royal Knights' mantles feature a train. The heraldic shield is worn on the left shoulder. The hat, a Tudor bonnet in black velvet, is decorated with a plume of white ostrich and black heron feathers.

A collar is worn over the mantle, around the neck, and is tied in bows on the shoulders with white ribbons. Suspended from the collar is The Great George, a likeness of the saint on horseback slaying the dragon. The Garter itself, a buckled dark blue velvet strap, is worn around the left calf by knights.

Under the mantle the Prince of Wales wore the traditional Tudor-style under-dress comprising white silk embroidered doublet, breeches, full hose or stockings, white doeskin pumps with satin bows and a sword on a sword belt.

H.R.H. THE PRINCE OF WALES, K.G.

COPYRIGHT PHOTO BY
D. KNIGHTS WHITTOME,
SUTTON & EPSOM

Coronation robes

Rules for peers and peeresses

October 14, 1936

Indications of rank

Three announcements by the Duke of Norfolk, Earl Marshal, with reference to the attendance of peers and peeresses at the coronation of King Edward VIII, and the dress regulations with which they will be required to conform, appear in last night's issue of the *London Gazette*.

The following is the text of the three announcements, each issued from the Earl Marshal's Office, 8 Buckingham Gate. SW1, under date October 12, and signed "Norfolk, Earl Marshal" –

Letters of summons

The King's Most Excellent Majesty having been pleased to command me, as Earl Marshal of England, to prepare and countersign letters to be passed under the Royal Sign Manual, requiring the attendance of the Peers and Peeresses of Great Britain at the solemnity of the Royal Coronation of His Majesty, and the King having been further pleased to command me to prepare such letters also for those Peers of Ireland whose right to vote at the election of a representative Peer for Ireland has, on claim made on their behalf, been admitted by the House of Lords and who are not now Members of the House of Commons, I do hereby request that all those Peers who, in conformity with the above regulations, are entitled to assist at the solemnity of the Royal Coronation of His Majesty, will be pleased to transmit their respective addresses to me at this office; and that the Dowager Peeresses and Peeresses who desire to attend at the said Coronation, will be also pleased to transmit their respective Christian names and addresses to me, in order that their letters of summons may be prepared without delay.

NOTE: *Only those Peers and Peeresses who reply to the above intimation before the first day of December, 1936, will receive the Royal Command to attend the Ceremony of the Coronation. It is to be understood that the above Orders refer to all English, Scottish and Irish Peers (except Peers who are minors and Irish Peers who have seats in the House of Commons), Peeresses in their own right, the widows of Peers, and the wives of living Peers, including the wives of Irish Peers who have seats in the House of Commons.*

Widows of Peers who have remarried under the rank of the Peerage are not entitled to such summons.

Peers' robes and coronets

The Earl Marshal's Order concerning the Robes, Coronets &c., which are to be worn by the Peers at the Coronation of His Most Sacred Majesty King Edward the Eighth. These are to give notice to all Peers who attend at the Coronation of His Majesty that the robe or mantle of the Peers be of crimson velvet, edged with miniver, the cape furred with miniver pure and powdered with bars or rows of ermine (i.e., narrow pieces of black fur), according to their degree, viz:

Barons, two rows.
Viscounts, two rows and a half.
Earls, three rows.
Marquesses, three rows and a half.
Dukes, four rows.

The said mantles or robes to be worn over full Court dress, uniform, or regimentals. The coronets to be of silver gilt; the caps of crimson velvet turned up with ermine, with a gold tassel on the top; and no jewels or precious stones are to be set or used in the coronets, or counterfeit pearls instead of silver balls.

The coronet of a Baron to have, on the circle or rim, six silver balls at equal distances.

The coronet of a Viscount to have, on the circle, sixteen silver balls.

The coronet of an Earl to have, on the circle, eight silver balls, raised upon points, with gold strawberry leaves between the points.

The coronet of a Marquess to have, on the circle, four gold strawberry leaves and four silver balls alternately, the latter a little raised on points above the rim. The coronet of a Duke to have, on the circle, eight gold strawberry leaves.

NOTE: *A Peer whose highest dignity is in the Peerage of Scotland or Ireland will wear robes and coronet of such dignity.*

Dress of peeresses

The Earl Marshal's Order concerning the Robes, &c., which are to be worn by the Peeresses at the Coronation of His Most Sacred Majesty King Edward the Eighth. These are to give notice to all Peeresses who attend at the Coronation of His Majesty that the robes or mantles appertaining to their respective ranks are to be worn over the usual full Court dress. That the robe or mantle of a Baroness be of crimson velvet, the cape thereof to be furred with miniver pure, and powdered with two bars or rows of ermine (i.e., narrow pieces of black fur); the said mantle to be edged round with miniver pure two inches in breadth, and the train to be three feet on the ground. That the robe or mantle of a Viscountess be like that of a Baroness, the cape to be powdered with two rows and a half of ermine, the edging of the mantle two inches as before, and the train a yard and a quarter. That the robe or mantle of a Countess be as before, the cape to be powdered with three rows of ermine, the edging three inches in breadth, and the train a yard and a half. That the robe or mantle of a Marchioness be as before, the cape to be powdered with three rows and a half of ermine, the edging four inches in breadth, the train a yard and threequarters. That the robe or mantle of a Duchess be as before; the cape to be powdered with four rows of ermine, the edging five inches broad, the train two yards.

NOTE: *The wives or widows of Peers, and Peeresses in their own right, whose highest dignity is in the Peerage of Scotland or Ireland, will wear robes of such dignity.*

The precedence of the widow of a Peer who has remarried with a Peer of lower degree is that of her last husband.

HAPPY AND GLORIOUS !

Left: At the coronation of her father George VII, an 11-year-old Princess Elizabeth waves from the balcony with her mother, the newly crowned Queen Elizabeth. It was originally planned that the young princesses would wear crimson velvet coronets edged in ermine, but they were deemed too heavy. Lightweight silver-gilt coronets in the style of medieval crowns were commissioned instead. As heir to the throne the princess had a slightly longer train than her sister Princess Margaret Rose, which caused a small upset in the nursery.

Above: Queen Elizabeth wears the Imperial Crown, which weighs 2.3lbs (1.06kg), waving from the Buckingham Palace balcony on her coronation, June 2, 1953. She was 27 years of age.

Imperial emblems on the Queen's dress

Tudor roses and plants from the Commonwealth

From our correspondent *June 2, 1953*

The emblems of Great Britain and the Commonwealth are embroidered on the gown which the Queen will wear in Westminster Abbey today. This is in white satin, with a fitted bodice and the neckline cut square over the shoulders and then curving into a heart shape. The sleeves are short and the skirt is only slightly trained. The bodice, sleeves, and hem of the skirt are bordered with an embroidered band of golden crystals, graduated diamonds, and pearls. Three similar bands across the skirt enclose emblems of each country represented. The emblems themselves form a garland against a latticework of seed pearl and crystal with which the gown is entirely encrusted.

The Tudor rose of England appears on the short sleeve, embroidered in palest pink silk, pearls, and gold and silver. In the first portion of the skirt the leek of Wales is shown, the leek flower being embroidered in white silk and diamonds, and the leaves in palest green silk. The second portion of the skirt shows the shamrock of Ireland in soft green silk, silver thread, and diamonds. The thistle of Scotland is represented in the third portion of the skirt, embroidered in pale mauve silk and amethysts. The calyx is embroidered in reseda-green silk, silver thread, and diamond dewdrops. Finally, in the last and widest part of the skirt, every emblem of the Commonwealth is shown closely surrounding the Tudor rose of England.

Tudor roses form a central motif of a mixed bouquet of emblematic flowers, clustered around which are further emblems. Canada is represented by the maple leaf embroidered in green silk, bordered with gold thread and veined in crystal. The wattle flower of Australia is shown with yellow blossom, the foliage in green and gold thread. Soft green silk again appears in the embroidery of the fern of New Zealand, which is veined with silver and crystal. The protea, emblematic flower of South Africa, appears in shaded pink silk, each petal bordered with silver thread. The leaves are shaded green silk and embellished with rose diamonds. The lotus flower of India has mother-of-pearl embroidered petals, with seed pearls and diamonds. Three emblems represent Pakistan: wheat, shown in oat-shaped diamonds with fronds of golden crystal; jute, in a spray of leaves of green silk and golden thread; and the cotton flower blossom, with stalks of silver and leaves of green silk. The lotus flower of Ceylon appears in white sequins, mother of pearl, diamonds, and soft green silk.

Above: The coronation dress, which weighed 30lbs (14kg), went with Queen Elizabeth II on her five-and-a-half month Commonwealth Tour. It was worn in each location no matter what the temperature. Here the Queen wears it in Australia, February 1954. She wears Queen Alexandra's Russian Kokoshnik Tiara and Queen Victoria's diamond collet necklace. Prince Philip wears the uniform of the Admiral of the Fleet.

Below: The Coronation dress is a garment that has to be seen to be believed. It is so firmly structured and then encrusted with shimmering and luminescent crystals and pearls that it seems almost armoured. It was exhibited at Buckingham Palace in 2016.

Left with nothing to wear

From our correspondent *May 10, 1977*

I had not realised until yesterday what a sadly underdressed affair this Silver Jubilee would be. The occasion was the opening of the exhibition Moss Bros have staged to mark the event. It shows a complete range of peers' coronation robes, plus a few extra trappings, such as royal heralds' and Beefeaters' costumes.

The show had to be coronation robes, Moss Bros explained, because there is no special finery to be donned for the jubilee.

Nor are the coronation robes on show ever likely to be worn. The peers' velvets, the firm estimated, cost at least

Post-war austerity was reflected in some "budget" styles exhibited at Norman Hartnell's atelier in Bruton Street, Mayfair, in January 1953 ahead of the coronation in June. As well as the "austerity cape" peeresses could consider a new cap of state costing £4 as an alternative to a £60 coronet.

£1,000 that year each. The peeresses', complete with the longer train Norman Hartnell introduced when economizing on the coronets in 1953, now cost twice as much.

The velvet robes are only worn at coronations but next time, Moss Bros calculate, economies are likely to go much further than the mere substitution of a cap of state for the old-time coronet. For one thing, the aristocracy are unlikely to be able to lay hands on anything to wear underneath their robes.

"At the last coronation we did 400 or 500 suits of velvet court dress at £25 for the day," confided Ted Eyers of the uniform department: "But we ran short of velvet, and now they have all been cut up for hunting caps. We made more money that way." Eyers recalls nostalgically the glory of jubilees past: "We were up all night for George VI's in 1935," he reminisced, "polishing brass buttons and breast plates. And we had all the gold braid to clean with cyanide

and a toothbrush. There will be nothing like that now."

At the Queen's coronation you could hire robe and coronet for £50. "We had rows and rows of big tin boxes with labels on the sides," Eyers said. "People started getting kitted out a year before." Now the hire fee would be at least £250, but the exhibition robes, made specially for this exhibition, are unlikely ever to enter Westminster Hall."

"Mostly they go for special exhibitions in Australia and Japan", said a senior Moss Bros employee. "They are very keen on such things in those countries, and it is funny how they just tend to disappear. Of course some others are disposed of through our theatrical costumes subsidiary. They have a demand for all sorts of things." By the time the next coronation comes around, Moss Bros guessed gloomily, peers might be reduced to wearing their parliamentary robes, mere superfine wool cloth as compared with genuine velvet.

Kings' crowns fell into private hands

Mystery of 40-year gap leaves heritage exposed to foreign sale

By Dalya Alberge   *December 4, 1995*

As a battle royal began yesterday to keep two historic crowns in Britain, there was bewilderment over why they had not been kept safe in the Tower of London.

The imperial state crown of George I is valued at £576,000 and the coronation crown of George IV at £376,000. But their importance to the national heritage is almost priceless. The state crown, thought to date from 1715, was adapted for the coronations of George II and William IV and as the state crown of George III and George IV. State crowns were used at the opening of Parliament and Victoria is believed to have used George I's regalia in the first year of her reign.

Asprey Antiques has acquired the crowns from a private collection and has made applications for their export. Charles Truman, a director, said: "I cannot think of anything more central to our heritage than the crowns of England. Our principal concern is that they should remain in this country, but as a commercial organisation we have a duty to our shareholders and owners."

Mr Truman said that the crowns appear to have been held until 1838 by the royal goldsmiths, Bridge and Rundell. "When they closed down in the early 1840s, it seems that the crowns were quietly disposed of, for reasons one can only guess at now."

There was a 40-year gap in which their whereabouts were unknown. In 1887 they were acquired by Lord Amherst of Hackney, a bibliophile. A correspondent of *The World* who visited his library expressed amazement at seeing there the crowns which "everyone else innocently believed to be safe in the Tower of London".

From 1935 to 1985 they were on loan to Kensington Palace and the Museum of London. Mr Truman said that his firm had bought the crowns from a private person in Britain, not the present Lord Amherst. Part of the crowns' importance lay in the fact that they reflected the state of the monarchy in the eighteenth century, when even the Royal Family had to rent its jewels, he said. "Until South African diamonds came on line and Indian princes gave them stones, they did not have the riches they have today." Consequently the crowns contain no jewels today, as the succession of monarchs hired the gems they required for the designs and uses to which they adapted them.

Historic Royal Palaces, the government agency which manages the Tower of London, is looking to the Victoria and Albert Museum for help in buying the crowns. Richard Edgcumbe, curator of jewellery at the Victoria

and Albert Museum, said: "The story of the Crown Jewels cannot seriously be told without these two crowns. They were central to the most important ceremonies of British constitutional Government, the coronation of the monarch and the opening of Parliament. They are evocative and beautiful objects, of outstanding importance to the study of jewellery, and they should be displayed in the Tower of London, their natural home."

David Barrie, director of the National Art Collections Fund, said: "If any objects deserve to stay in this country, then these surely do. The crowns are so hugely evocative of our history and such splendid items of royal regalia that it would be a tragedy if they were to go overseas." The state crown of George I was modified in 1727 for the coronation of George II, when it was set with hired diamonds, and was used throughout his reign for the opening of Parliament. When George III acceded to the throne, it was cleaned and altered to fit his head.

Until the reign of George III, the crown was displayed with the other crown jewels in the Tower of London when not in use. The only crown that is more significant, according to the V&A, is the 1661 St Edward's crown in the Tower, which regained its role as the coronation crown in 1911.

Robes and finery are just what this drab world needs

By Melanie McDonagh

May 4, 2023

So, how do you feel about the flummery of the coronation? How about the crimson velvet robe of state that the King begins the service with? The supertunica, made from cloth of gold? Or, the pièce de résistance, the robe royal, or imperial mantle, a heavy gold cloak made for George IV, embroidered heavily with fleurs-de-lys? That's before we get to the jewelled sword. And the crown. And the purple velvet robe of estate in which Charles III leaves the Abbey.

I love it. For in this drab egalitarian world, the pomp evokes all the things that kingship should be synonymous with: splendour, magnificence, pomp and circumstance. They don't pertain to Charles himself but to the monarchy, that anachronistic and counter-cultural institution. And if the pomp seems out of place in the modern world, good. For we've got to a sad point in our history where wealth and power are no longer expressed in cloth of gold and costly velvet – unless you're at the Met Gala. Our billionaires wear T-shirts and jeans, like Mark Zuckerberg; the least they could do to raise our spirits is flaunt apes and peacocks.

Display is essentially life-enhancing, a way for ordinary folk to enjoy the glittering ostentation of the great. Historically, it has always been so.

The newly-crowned King Charles III travels back to Buckingham Palace in the Imperial Crown after his coronation, May 6, 2023.

Resplendent in a red plume

By Lucy Bannerman

May 7, 2023

No one could accuse the Princess Royal of underdressing for the occasion. For a woman who has spent her entire life being bumped further and further down the line of succession, first by her younger brothers, then by her brothers' children and grandchildren, while appearing not in the least bit bothered about it, she still managed to make her own mark at the coronation.

As "Gold Stick in Waiting", Anne had one of the strangest roles on a day that was not short of peculiar ceremony. When the new king emerged from Westminster Abbey, it was Anne who rode on horseback behind him, entrusted to protect his personal safety with her gold-headed ebony staff.

To be fair, she did have the back-up of 29,000 police officers, not to mention the security services, but her official role as the King's personal bodyguard was a sign of the monarch's respect for his sister, as a confidante and defender of his reign.

Who could have been more suited to the role than Anne, whose memorable response to the armed man who tried to kidnap her on the same stretch of the Mall almost 50 years ago was: "Not bloody likely"?

She spoke about her duties in an interview with Canadian Television last week. "I have a role as the Colonel of the Blues and Royals in the Household Cavalry regiment as Gold Stick [in Waiting]. And Gold Stick was the original close protection officer," she said.

The role of Gold Stick in Waiting can be traced to the Tudor era, when fears of a conspiracy against Henry VIII prompted an increase in his personal security. "That is a role I was asked if I'd like to do for this coronation, so I said yes," Anne said: "Not least of all, it solves my dress problem."

It certainly did. Not for Anne high heels and a fascinator. She arrived resplendent in a remarkable pointed hat with a red plume, which just so happened to obscure the face of the most controversial guest, her nephew, Harry, who was sitting behind her.

Once the ceremony was over, the 72-year-old grandmother of five appeared calm and confident as she emerged on horseback to lead all the Household Division regiments from Westminster Abbey to Buckingham Palace. "So relaxed in the saddle," said Clare Balding, the broadcaster and fellow horsewoman, admiringly.

Let's Crown Kate now! She's got the star power

By Hilary Rose　　　　　　　　　　　　　　　*May 8, 2023*

Can you be sent to the Tower for saying that the Princess of Wales is slaying it? I'll risk my neck, because at the coronation there was no other word. She played her part spectacularly well. If ever a woman faced a date with destiny, it was her. If ever a woman rose to it, she did. When rumours started circulating a week or so ago that she was going to wear flowers in her hair, I thought: "Oh no. Please don't. It's a coronation, not Woodstock." I needn't have worried.

The Princess of Wales knows exactly what she's doing. As of this weekend there is no longer any trace of the slightly nervy, unremarkable middle-class girl from the home counties. Somewhere along the way Kate Middleton has acquired more star power and charisma and regal bearing than all the other royals combined. How ironic that Prince Andrew bangs on about his "blood princess" daughters, but it's actually the girl from Berkshire who makes the monarchy look exciting and relevant. You can tell me till you're blue in the face that the monarchy isn't about star power, that it's about stability, the constitution, yada yada blah. It is and it isn't, but star power matters. Henry VIII knew it. Elizabeth I knew it and so did Elizabeth II. Now it matters more than ever, in the internet age when civilian stars are ten a penny, as Harry and Meghan are discovering, but royal fairy dust is thin on the ground.

There's a photograph of her arriving at the abbey and looking over her shoulder directly into the camera. Compare it to one taken in the same place on her wedding day and see the transformation. There's a steeliness to her gaze that wasn't there 12 years ago. There's an alchemy at work that the other royals must desperately wish they could bottle.

And Kate's 3D-embroidered headpiece was a modern masterstroke. No one can compete with the Crown Jewels – which, as she's well aware, she'll be wearing next time around – so don't even try. In the meantime she'd clearly decided to shake things up a bit. She ticked the Diana box with her earrings. She could have worn any tiara under the sun, but instead she wore that confection of silver bullion, crystals and silver thread, and hats off, as it were, to the milliner Jess Collett.

The new Princess of Wales wore an ivory silk crepe dress, designed by Alexander McQueen, to the coronation of King Charles III. It featured silver-bullion threadwork embroidery, depicting the rose, the shamrock, the thistle and the leek. It was largely covered by her Royal Victorian Order mantle which was made by Ede and Ravenscroft, London's oldest tailor and robe-maker, established in 1689.

GLAMOUR

Via the seductive artifice of glamorous eveningwear, the royal family embodies the notion that they are not like other mortals. The reality may be different, but the carefully curated, sparkling image fulfils our fantasies of royalty. They glitter, twinkle and shine in the work of (mostly) British designers and are adorned with the most fabulous baubles to complete the dazzling effect.

The slender and beautiful Queen Alexandra, born a Danish princess, fully embraced the concept of royal glamour. Cecil Beaton observed in has book *The Glass of Fashion*, that Edward VII's wife started the tradition that royalty could wear anything at any time of day and get away with it. She wore evening clothes in the day and piled on jewellery, including her trademark ropes of pearls around her neck to conceal a small scar.

On the death of Queen Elizabeth's mother (the Countess of Strathmore and Kinghorne) in 1938, Her Majesty needed a sudden change of wardrobe for a long-planned state visit to Paris. Mourning clothes were required, but this was an important visit and the Queen had to make an impact. Her husband George VI took her couturier Norman Hartnell to view the Winterhalter portraits in the Royal Collection and boldly suggested the opulent nineteenth-century costumes be used as inspiration.

"The royal visit to Paris is over but the memory of it will live long with all Parisians," enthused *The Times* fashion correspondent on July 22, 1938. "The splendour of the dresses worn at the three State dinner parties, at the Bagatelle garden party and for the luncheon at Versailles will not be forgotten quickly. Queen Elizabeth's wardrobe, designed in London, by Norman Hartnell and fashioned with French materials, was widely admired. "Loveliest of all were the crisp white lace frock which Her Majesty wore at the garden party, the panniered satin dress trimmed with silver lace and camellias in which she attended the Opera, and her white and silver brocade dress for the dinner at the Ministry of Foreign Affairs,".

By moving from contemporary style into costume and using an entirely white wardrobe (white being an alternative mourning colour), Hartnell created a majestic sensation.

Elizabeth II and her younger sister Princess Margaret shimmered through their twenties and thirties in a series of structured evening gowns in pretty sorbet shades by Hartnell, all nipped-in waists and full skirts, heavy with beading and embroidery. Seen up close these dresses are beautiful marvels of couture craftsmanship. One rare diversion by Queen Elizabeth II was the dramatic black velvet dress she wore to the Royal Film Performance of *The Battle of the River Plate* in 1957. In the cast line-up Her Majesty came face to face with Marilyn Monroe and succeeded in outshining her.

Elizabeth II, of course, had grown up in a world where exceptionally glamorous evening dresses were the norm. For royal newcomers this can be a difficult genre. The Emanuels' voluminous black taffeta frock the 19-year-old Lady Diana Spencer wore on her first public engagement revealed, as she leant to exit her car, a fabulous cleavage that caused camera bulbs to pop. Diana learnt as she matured, however, moving on from what she called her "fairy-tale evening dresses" to more svelte lines. The masterful "Revenge Dress" she wore in June 1994 the same night Prince Charles admitted adultery in a television interview was the ultimate sartorial statement.

Catherine, Princess of Wales, has a sure touch with eveningwear, displaying a firm grip on the essential rules: reveal a little skin, but not too much, and counterbalance figure-hugging frocks with decorous high necks and long sleeves. This is a fine line: royal glamour can be quietly seductive but it must not project sexiness.

The Duchess of Sussex, familiar with red-carpet dressing, demonstrates confident star quality. Meghan's eveningwear for royal functions showed an understated modernity, the pared-down American design influence dazzlingly stylish. She steered her way through the royal minefield with frocks free from glittering embellishment. Since stepping away from royal duties she has embraced a hint more Hollywood glamour with plunging necklines and thigh-high splits, though still remaining, in contemporary rather than royal terms, decorous.

H.R.H. PRINCESS MARY, VISCOUNTESS LASCELLES.

Compare and contrast the seismic shift in royal style in just 30 years.

Left: A tightly corseted Princess Alexandra is leaving no doubt as to her royal status circa 1890. She is frilled, beaded, swathed in tulle, trimmed with lace and awash with jewels. She is wearing the Dagmar Necklace, a gift from King Frederick VII of Denmark on her marriage to Edward, Prince of Wales. The necklace had 118 pearls and 2,000 diamonds. She has orders pinned on her breast and a circlet on her head.

Above: Princess Mary is photographed shortly after her marriage to Viscount Lascelles in 1922. There is no corset and her dress is dropped waist, loose and flowing. She is wearing the Diamond Scroll Tiara.

111 J   H.M. QUEEN MARY.   BEAGLES' POSTCARDS

Queen Mary is photographed early in her reign dripping with jewels and wearing a heavily beaded dress, Edwardian in style. She is wearing her pearl and diamond dog collar, as well as five ropes of pearls, and her tiara with upstanding pearls.

Queen Elizabeth twinkles and sparkles in beaded tulle in Buckingham Palace on New Year's Eve, 1938. Couturier Norman Hartnell created the dress for Her Majesty's state visit to France earlier in the year and it is easy to see why she created such a sensation in his designs.

Left: The Duchess of Windsor shows off her playful side in this specially commissioned silk organza dress from Givenchy. As the Duchess requested, it was embroidered with monkeys playing musical instruments. She was photographed at the Waldorf Astoria Towers Royal Suite in 1954, where she and the Duke spent part of every year between 1951 and 1960.

Above: Wallis Simpson wears a simple Mainbocher sequinned jacket and white crepe dress with a matching sequin sash. Photographed here in May 1937, she is displaying her whopping emerald engagement ring a month before her marriage to the Duke of Windsor. After her death the ring was sold by Sotheby's for £1.9 million.

Magnificent Marina

Photographed in March 1944, almost 18 months after the death of her husband George, Duke of Kent, in a plane crash in August 1942, Princess Marina shows that less is more. Always understated, she liked simple and elegant silhouettes.

Photographed here by Cecil Beaton in 1937, in a dress so clean lined and simple one could imagine any royal stepping out in it today.

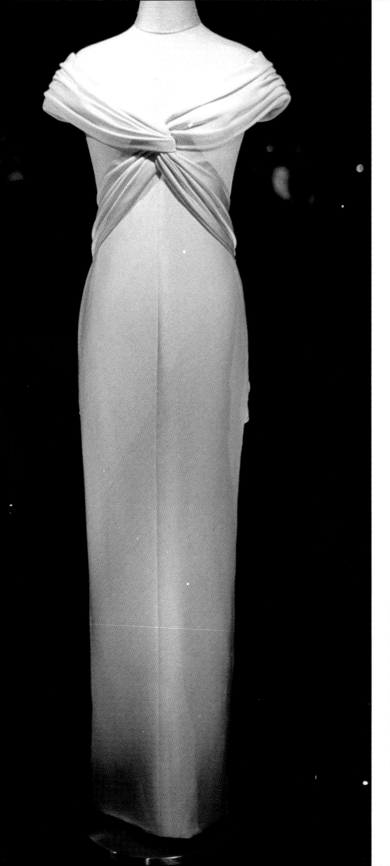

Specialising in bespoke
eveningwear, Catherine
Walker designed this
deceptively simple cream
silk-crepe twist-front evening
dress for Diana, Princess of
Wales. It was first worn at a
state banquet for the King
and Queen of Malaya in
1993. It was sold at Christie's
auction in 1997 for $52,900.

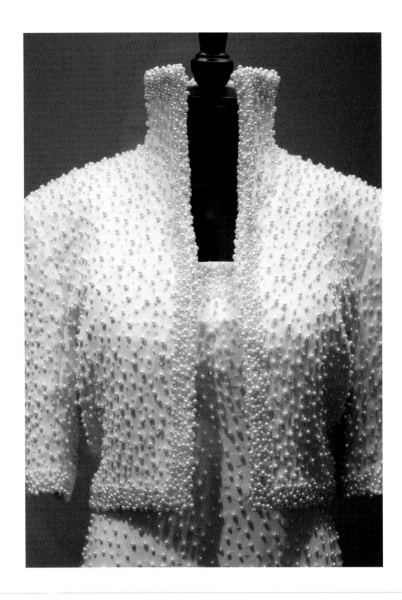

Dubbed the 'Elvis dress' by both Diana, Princess of Wales, and the fashion press – its high stand-up collar was reminiscent of one of Elvis Presley's famous stage costumes – this silk dress and jacket by Catherine Walker relies on texture to create an impact. Both the slim column strapless dress and the bolero are encrusted with sequins and oyster pearls. The dress was commissioned for an official visit to Hong Kong in November 1989, the beading work was undertaken by the British firm S. Lock Ltd which sewed on almost 30,000 pearl beads. The princess wore it for the first time to the British Fashion Awards a month earlier. Walker was up for the British Glamour Award at the event, but didn't win. Diana's sensational outfit was a timely reminder of the incredible skills of this clever designer and Walker went on to win the award in 1991. It was sold at Christie's auction for $151,000.

Frocks and rocks

Nobody does eveningwear better than Her Majesty

By Sarah Mower   *April 17, 2016*

Can it be a coincidence that we're witnessing an outbreak of floor-length capes, tiaras and golden decorations in the spring of 2016, or is something in the collective fashion-unconscious paying homage to Her Majesty the Queen in all her splendour? It's a thought that has floated past my field of vision more than once as I've been scribbling the word "regal" at Alexander McQueen, Valentino, Saint-Laurent, Gucci and Dries Van Noten recently. If so, well, hurrah!

It's the Queen's long history of dressing for evening and high state occasions that is suddenly looking inspirationally fashionable. That marks a turn-up for the books that would have raised the eyebrows, if not the hackles, of Sir Norman Hartnell at the beginning of her reign. "The Queen and the Queen Mother do not want to be fashion setters. That's left to other people with less important work to do," the royal couturier remarked in an exquisitely English slap-down to a *New York Times* reporter, who was excited to learn about the 27-year-old Queen's dresses for her Commonwealth tour in 1953.

From the start, the beautiful young fairy-tale Queen had an in-built distrust of being judged as fashionable, and she set out as she meant to go on. At the beginning, there was a royal fear of being seen as extravagant in post-war Britain, and of course there was the dreadful family spectre of that wrecker of an American fashion plate, Wallis Simpson, still lurking in the background.

But there was a lot more to it than that. Nancy Mitford's acerbically witty observation of the contrasts between English, French and American chic nailed the explanation for the American readers of *The Atlantic Monthly* in 1951. Among English society women since the beginning of the century, she wrote, "nothing was considered so common as to be dressed in the height of fashion".

Women in the streets of London habitually dressed drearily. Yet, she declared, "These same women at a ball are a surprise and a delight. In the evening, they excel. With their beautiful jewels glittering on their beautiful skins, with their absolute unselfconsciousness ... they are unbeatable. There is no more dazzling sight than a ball at Buckingham Palace." Does anything better sum up the Queen's lifelong position vis-à-vis keeping fashion at arm's length while upholding the British monarchy?

In the wondrous formal world of evening occasions, state banquets, balls, family parties and openings of parliament, she has been free to be her one and only, supreme Queen-like self, all insignia, diamonds and tiaras blazing. As Mitford put it, it's this "unbeatable" Queen Elizabeth II who is the fascination of fashion now.

One night, in Paris, she sailed down the Seine in a silver bugle-beaded dress and a white fox-fur cape and magnificent jewels. Speaking in the stronghold of Parisian haute couture – which had never heard of Hartnell – her designer persisted in the pretence that this wasn't fashion at all. "The Queen is not much interested in fashion," he said to the press. "She likes to be comfortable." Amies, meanwhile, chortled over the British score against the French fashion establishment. "The Frogs may have the frocks, but we've got the rocks."

Far from the last time the Queen has worn a British-designed, British-made formal long dress of some pale or gleaming material, typically with a richly embroidered bodice, though. These days, Angela Kelly's shapes are still the simplified versions of the column dresses the Queen started wearing in the 1960s. For all state occasions, banquets and jubilees, that is what we see her in. It's the look she owns, her regal triumph over fashion.

Queen Elizabeth II at 41 could still outshine everyone else. Here she wears a heavily beaded column evening dress. The Queen Victoria diamond collet necklace and earrings help to no end, as does the Queen Mary's Girls of Great Britain and Ireland Tiara. She is swathed in white mink and over her white evening gloves she wears a diamond bracelet and a diamond and platinum watch.

Above: The new Queen Elizabeth, photographed at Buckingham Palace in 1953, wears a strapless white tulle evening dress with a fine silver lace overlay. On her head she wears the Diamond Diadem, a nineteenth-century diamond fringe necklace and on her sash, the smallest piece of Queen Mary's Stomacher. The Duke of Edinburgh is wearing the uniform of Admiral of the Fleet.

Right: This Norman Hartnell dress created for Queen Elizabeth II in the 1950s highlights the skill and craftsmanship of this couture house. Hartnell understood embellishment and his exquisitely constructed dresses transformed a beautiful young woman into an impressive symbol of pomp and power. This dress was exhibited at Buckingham Palace in 2006.

Coming out of the closet

By Angela Huth *October 5, 1986*

Members of the royal family, subjected to the constant critical glare of publicity, can never get by with throwing on an unconsidered garment and hoping it won't be noticed. It will. For the royal family are always on show, always vulnerable to criticism, always having to think about what clothes will work.

Princess Margaret admits that clothes are important to her but not one of her greatest priorities, and she sets about her wardrobe with practical zest, unfailing stamina and considerable humour.

"The careful planning, the fittings – they're all part of one's life," says the Princess. "You even get used to all those fittings; after a while, it's a bit like going to the dentist. I've learned never to have too long a fitting, or you begin to droop. I plan twice a year: summer things and winter things. Once that's over I put it all out of my mind unless I suddenly realise I haven't the right thing for the right occasion. Then I just have to try to fudge it, try to get away with putting things together that I already have."

"I can rarely dress for fun. I have very few home clothes, mostly working clothes. My working clothes are like most people's best clothes. I wear last year's for some private occasions, but they're too grand for the country. I always, always have to be practical. I can't have skirts too tight because of getting in and out of cars and going up steps. Sleeves can't be too tight either: they must be all right for waving. Then I can't have anything that crushes too much – linen, for example. Back views are very important. Most people don't think about their backs, but, as I'm going to be seen from all directions, I have to have things that photograph well. I have to think about change of temperature: long coats and dresses are more useful than suits. You can take the coat off when you arrive inside and be dressed up underneath. But you can't very well take off the coat of a suit and go about in just a shirt on an official occasion."

Despite considerable additions to her wardrobe every year, the princess likes to keep old favourites for a long time and wears them often. She has a facecloth cloak, for instance, of brilliant peacock blue, made for her at Sarah Spencer. "So useful. I wear it over and over again. I hope it will go on and on." Looking back, she vividly remembers many favourite dresses (several of which she has donated to the Victoria and Albert Museum). They include a pink and grey dress made by Jean Dessés in the fifties: the jacket could be taken off to transform it into a short evening dress.

Another much-loved dress, in which the Princess was photographed on her 18th birthday, was of pale blue grosgrain, made by Norman

Hartnell; the epitome of the New Look, which Princess Margaret particularly loved. Hartnell ("always so good at getting the balance right") was also the maker of another favourite evening dress – an enormous tulle skirt embroidered with iridescent butterflies. "But my favourite dress of all was never photographed. It was my first Dior dress, white strapless tulle and a vast satin bow at the back."

In the fifties she was "taken in hand" by Lady Jean Rankin, lady-in-waiting to the Queen. "It was Jean who introduced me to Rene, the hairdresser, and also to Simone Mirman, from whom I got my hats for many years." These days, clothes are acquired from a number of sources. For a foreign tour, she says, there is usually too much to do for one designer, so she goes to several.

"Obviously, abroad, I like to wear English things – Caroline Charles, for instance. Sally Crewe at Sarah Spencer is very kind as she brings me shapes, then does them in special materials. She did a lot for my tour to Denmark last year. And she also made me something I've always longed for, a short evening dress that can

also be long. It's made from a scarlet and gold sari, with a separate long underskirt, so I can wear it either way. Very useful." Roger Brines, a Frenchman over here, has been designing clothes for the princess for many years – he produced the azalea dress she wore at the Prince and Princess of Wales's wedding. For really special occasions she sometimes persuades her old friend Carl Toms, the theatrical designer, to think up something for her. "Carl has me absolutely right. He's used to small people because of designing for ballet dancers." If she finds she has nothing for private occasions she "really shops around," going to all sorts of places for things off the peg.

Princess Margaret loves dressing up for evenings, and also for Ascot. "I get four new things every year for Ascot, although I can usually manage to get away without four new evening dresses, too." Materials for the evening she likes to be "all the richest: velvets, satins, silks –but not much decolletage, these days. I think when you're older exposing too much skin is hideous."

Nowadays, as always, the Princess says she likes London clothes better than

country ones. "I don't ever wear trousers, but skirts and jerseys or shirts in the country, or tweeds with long coats or macs. What I really like best in the day are dresses." She has a good collection of these, many in fine, printed wools, very simple and comfortable. "In the evening in private life I'm very unfashionable in that I wear long dresses when most people are wearing short, but it's because I've got so many long ones." She has firm views about the decline of the old evening ritual of changing. "People no longer seem to have a sense of occasion. My feeling is that if you're going out in the evening then you want to have a bath and change into clean clothes: you choose something to suit the occasion. To me, smartness is not only to do with clothes, but make-up, hair, bags, jewellery, even nails. They all add up to the finished effect."

The princess has few definite dislikes. "I never wear brown, I find it very depressing. I don't much like purple, either, though I like refinements of that colour. I can't bear materials that aren't smooth – boucle or shaggy tweed – and I never wear silk crepe. I know a low waist doesn't suit me, and I'm not a very frilly person.

Hats mean I'm on duty, and anyway I'm convinced I look ridiculous in a hat. For formal occasions, of course, I have to wear hats, often to match whatever else I'm wearing. Many of them come from Graham Smith."

"I'm always conscious of what's in fashion," she says, "because without following it too strictly, one must get the line right. What I really enjoy is seeing how clothes are constructed: finding out how things are made and what of, and I enjoy going to dress shows." She loves seeing women in pretty clothes, and two whose clothes she much admires are the Duchess of Kent and the Duchess of Buccleuch. "They're both marvellous coat hangers. They could put on any old thing and look wonderful."

Princess Margaret admits to being a conventional dresser. "I dress for the public," she says. "I have to conform. I care about clothes but I've never thought of myself as a leader of fashion." For many years she was the victim of fashion writers, however, who, generation after generation, pick upon various members of the Royal Family and criticise their ways of dressing.

Looking back, Princess Margaret sees this trait as a recurring pattern, part of which used to include her, and from which she suffered. "In an interview on television last year the Princess of Wales said all the things I was saying 25 years ago. Clothes aren't her prime concern. They weren't mine. But the fashion writers persist in treating her, as they did me, as if we were just unreal figures straight from *Dynasty*."

Despite the criticism, Princess Margaret has continued very much in her own way over the years – in her own words, "always consistent in a limited fashion, always aware of a sense of occasion. I merely always try to look my best because that's a kind of compliment to those who have invited you to something, or who are around you. It's the least you can do." As for being complimented herself on her clothes? The Princess laughs merrily. "Well, when that happens it's very nice. It gives one confidence."

Left: Princess Margaret tries out a new silhouette in 1958, showing off her figure in this slim Norman Hartnell evening dress with full tulle overskirt front and back.

Previous Page: An oyster tulle Christian Dior evening dress with gold embroidery and beading, designed for Princess Margaret for her 21st birthday. It was exhibited at the *Christian Dior: Designer of Dreams* exhibition at London's Victoria and Albert Museum in 2019.

Princess Margaret's twentieth-birthday gown is of rich satin, with cascades of roses.
The cuff-neckline is also adorned with roses. Her necklace is of five strands of pearls

PHOTOGRAPHED BY BARON

Above: A 20-year-old Princess Margaret attends a ball at the Hurlingham Club in June 1951. She is wearing a pale blue and pink silk-satin Norman Hartnell evening dress embellished with giant satin flowers in soft pastel shades. The over-the-top saccharine sweetness of this dress is perfect for a young princess.

Right: Princess Margaret displays the power of a Hartnell dress as she sweeps down a staircase for a state dinner in British Honduras in 1958. Such a display of opulent magnificence is designed to impress.

Right: Princess Anne in typically no-frills style attends the world premiere of *Run Wild, Run Free* in London's Leicester Square in 1969. This crisp and architectural evening coat and dress was very suitable for the 18-year-old princess.

Far Right: It is hard to see the impact of this silk chiffon Ian Thomas dress, designed for Queen Elizabeth II, in a still photograph. In the 1970s Thomas produced a series of soft chiffon dresses for her, not too fussy for a mature woman, but the fabric, light as a whisper, shifts and moves in the smallest breeze. This dress was exhibited in the *Fashioning a Reign* exhibition at Windsor Castle in 2016.

The Revenge Dress

On June 29, 1994, Princess Diana sprang from her limo and walked briskly into a gala dinner hosted by *Vanity Fair* at the Serpentine Gallery. The photographer Tim Graham recalled that it took her around 30 seconds to cover the ground between the car and the gallery entrance, but nevertheless her brief appearance caused a worldwide sensation.

She was not scheduled to attend the gala, having initially declined the invitation, but is reported to have changed her mind a few days earlier. Instead of hiding from public view on the night Prince Charles's interview with Jonathan Dimbleby, in which he confessed adultery, was broadcast, she not only stood her ground but delivered a sartorial slap. Her choice of dress had such a seismic impact that it blasted Charles from the next day's front pages with wall-to-wall coverage of what the press dubbed "The Revenge Dress". In her 2007 book *The Diana Chronicles*, Tina Brown revealed that fashion editors described it as her "f**k you" dress. Journalist and author Georgina Howell described it as "possibly the most strategic dress ever worn by a woman in modern times" in her 1998 book *Diana, Her Life in Fashion*.

The dress, which later appeared in the Christie's auction sale of her dresses in New York on June 25, 1997, sold for $74,000, rather more than the £900 she had paid for it in 1991.

Christina Stambolian, the designer of the dress, revealed in a Channel 4 documentary, *Princess Diana's Dresses: The Auction*, that Princess Diana had purchased the dress eight months earlier, but had never worn it, considering it "too daring". The dress was a last-minute switch from a Valentino number, which she rejected after the designer released a press statement revealing what she would wear, though her butler Paul Burrell maintains she made the switch in an effort to look her most devastating.

The off-the-shoulder figure-hugging dress was made from black silk damask, its bodice was crisscrossed with minute pleats and it had an asymmetric hemline and floating chiffon panels. It took two dressmakers 60 hours to make. In wearing a provocative black dress she held up two sartorial fingers to royal protocol and presented the world with a picture of radiant, independent strength.

Jane Eastoe

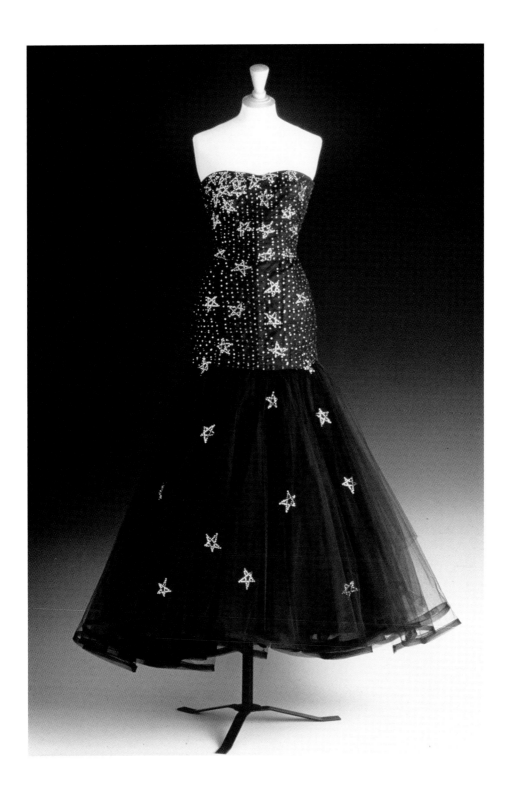

Far left: This midnight blue silk tulle strapless dress was designed by Murray Arbeid. Both bodice and skirt were adorned with diamante stars and the bodice was decorated with sequins so it twinkled. Diana, Princess of Wales, wore the dress to the London premiere of *Phantom of the Opera* in 1986. It was sold at the 1997 Christie's auction for $48,300.

Left: By 1986 Diana, Princess of Wales, was moving away from the full skirted, ruffled and frilled eveningwear of the early 1980s and was beginning to find her style feet. This shimmering, crystal beaded, silver and white one-shouldered silk chiffon dress by the Japanese designer Hachi was a gift from *Vogue* editor Anna Harvey. She wore it first to the Bond premiere of *License to Kill* in 1983 and is seen here in Washington in 1985.

Glamorous by anyone's standards

By Charlie Gowans-Eglinton

September 29, 2021

The on-trend caped shoulders, gold sequins cinching in the waist and following every curve, whopping gold earrings and perfect white smile: she was as glamorous, if not more so, than any Bond girl walking the red carpet. Even 007 Daniel Craig stopped to tell her that she looked "jolly lovely". Yet this was no A-list actress – it was the Duchess of Cambridge, our queen in waiting.

In the ten years since Kate Middleton's marriage into the royal family, her style has changed dramatically. She was in her late twenties then; she'll celebrate her 40th birthday in January and has had three children in the interim. Yet instead of her style ageing, if anything it has become more youthful, probably because for her first years as a duchess she took her cues from the Duchess of Cornwall and the Queen, both of whom are decades older. Her go-tos were smart dress coats from heritage British brands such as Catherine Walker in a rainbow of bright, cheery colours, much like the Queen, and elegant (ie covered up) evening dresses that, while glitzy, were always on the shoulder-pad side of conservative.

But this was sexy, and Hollywood, and properly glamorous. Not glamorous for a royal – glamorous by anyone's standards. Kate even looked more confident in it, her hand on Prince Charles's shoulder as they embraced, not overly deferential, but secure. The dress nodded a bit to the gold lamé that Princess Diana wore to a Bond premiere in 1985, but dialled-up the drama several notches.

It was a bespoke design created for Kate by Jenny Packham, but it's most similar to the designer's Elizabeth dress (£3,640). I'm guessing it wasn't named after Elizabeth II, who has never worn such a thing, but Elizabeth Taylor, and the jaw-dropping gold dress and cape that she wore to play Cleopatra: a reminder that when you're the queen, you can write your own dress code.

Left: Jenny Packham has produced some incredible evening dresses for the former Duchess of Cambridge, now Princess of Wales. This deep green tulle dress is delicately dotted with sequins and was worn at a dinner hosted by the Governor General of Jamaica in 2022. In a pale colour it might hint at fairy princess, but in this rich colour the Duchess of Cambridge looks simply magnificent and she gives a diplomatic nod to the Jamaican flag.

Above: This pale pink chiffon Jenny Packham dress with beading and paillettes was first worn to the 10th Annual ARK Gala dinner in 2011 but has been worn repeatedly since. As a new member of the royal family the Duchess of Cambridge keeps her look relaxed with long hair and minimal jewellery.

Above and right: There are some fail-safe looks that just work for royalty, as demonstrated here by Diana, Princess of Wales, and the Duchess of Cambridge. The style is classic and timeless. Diana's pale blue chiffon Catherine Walker dress with matching stole was worn numerous times, seen here at the Cannes Film Festival in 1997. It was sold at auction by Christie's for $70,700. Following Diana's lead, the new Duchess of Cambridge wears Alexander McQueen to the BAFTAS in July 2011.

Left: The Duchess of Sussex proves that elegance doesn't pause for pregnancy in a stark, black velvet Givenchy dress worn to attend the 2018 Fashion Awards.

Above: The Duchess of Sussex steps out in a clean-lined, decorous and absolutely fabulous red cape dress by Safiyaa in March 2020, with the overall impact heightened by towering red heels and the red Manolo Blahnik clutch.

AT PLAY

The ubiquitous advance of casualwear and sportswear in our everyday wardrobes over the last half-century has presented royalty with something of a style dilemma. How can they retain their regal dignity while embracing a more modern approach?

By following pursuits that once formed part of the season: yachting, horse racing, polo – indeed all and any equestrian sport – and the traditional country sports of hunting, shooting and fishing, they have been able to skirt the issue in a different kind of uniform. They are familiar sights in tweeds, waxed jackets, sensible waterproof footwear, topped off with tweed caps or headscarves, but this is hardly radical stuff.

The wearing of kilts and tartans, so enthusiastically promoted by the late Queen Mother, a Scot herself, clearly proclaimed the royals' partiality to all things Scottish while also effectively signalling that they were off duty and not to be disturbed.

Riding, racing and breeding fine equine specimens literally has been "the sport of kings" (and at least one queen) for centuries. The rigid dress codes still enforced at certain race meetings – hats and tails are still pre-requisite at Royal Ascot – require that, for once, the public dress to the nines like the royals. Thus their Royal Highnesses can enjoy their favourite pastime without standing out from the crowd.

Entering into the spirit of the occasion, bookies would take bets on what colour hat Queen Elizabeth II would wear to the races, so this decision was always made at the last moment. When the royals take to the field in sports such as polo and eventing, which they do so enthusiastically, they can again relax in clothes prescribed by regulation.

Her Majesty was very rarely seen in public in trousers, and then only for reasons of health and safety such as protection from insects and snakes. This article of clothing was strictly reserved for horse riding in private. When formal occasions required her to be on horseback in public she rode side saddle in uniform, with a tailored riding skirt, long after all other women had abandoned this practice. Despite being an inveterate hat wearer, she habitually resisted pressure to wear a hard hat when riding, opting for a headscarf instead to preserve her neatly sculpted hairdo.

Edward, Prince of Wales, later briefly Edward VIII, was a keen horseman with such a fearless attitude to point-to-point riding that his mother Queen Mary urged him to desist. On a tour of Canada in 1919, he famously leapt on to a horse in his lounge suit to the delight of his hosts home on the range.

Out of the saddle, his flamboyant personal style impacted on golf attire. He favoured patterned Fair Isle knitted sweaters, generously cut plus-fours, colourful argyle socks teamed with a soft flat cap and two-tone cleated shoes. It's a brave look, but nevertheless elements remain popular on the links today where normally conservative men still stride out in colourful argyll sweaters teamed with pastel separates way out of their normal comfort zone.

Edward VII's love of yachting stimulated a trend for wearing blazers and white trousers, a style similarly employed by his son, later George V, who looked shipshape off duty in a navy blazer and peaked cap.

Swimming presents a huge probem for royal women. While kings and princes can rush in and out of the waves like would-be action heroes, queens and princesses prefer to avoid such invasive personal scrutiny or opportunity for lascivious comment. Only the bravest are willing to do so. Sun-worshipper and royal rebel Princess Margaret was regularly snapped in structured bathing suits on Mustique. Princess Diana, uncomfortable in her own skin for years. was only latterly prepared to be seen in swimwear in a clear signal of self-confident liberation after exiting her marriage.

But then she did not start life as a royal and therefore, like Catherine, Princess of Wales and Meghan, Duchess of Sussex after her, slipping into casuals is no big deal. These are the clothes they can pick for themselves, that they can be confident in. Clothes they can run about in and clothes in which they can relate to you and me in a more real sense. It's captivating and they look good. No wonder we rush to follow their lead.

Shipshape and Bristol Fashion

Above: Queen Alexandra and her daughter Princess Victoria pose on board the Royal Yacht Victoria and Albert in 1908. Sailor style was clearly *de rigueur* on board ship.

Right: On board the royal yacht 13 years later Queen Mary and Princess Mary relax in cream suits and straw hats, a different kind of uniform with mother and daughter in perfect synchronicity. Queen Mary has embraced the wearing of the toque hat and despite being off duty she still has a whopping jewel pinned to her neck.

H.R.H. PRINCESS MARY

Left: Three years after their marriage the Duke and Duchess of York are photographed on board HMS Renown in 1927. The Duchess is all in white, wearing a loose, dropped-waist blouse and skirt, a matching lightweight coat, accessorised in best 1920s style with a cloche hat and a long string of pearls. The Duke looks very relaxed despite being in uniform.

Above: The exact date of this photograph is unknown, but Princess Mary was almost certainly a teenager when it was taken at some point in the 1910s. In a radical break from traditional court style she is wearing a soft pinafore dress with a collarless top. The laurel wreath hair ornament is faintly reminiscent of The Duchess of Cambridge's headpiece in the recent coronation. The silk shoes, perfectly poised to press the piano pedals, are exquisite.

Society's glamour duo

Far left: Princess Marina, Duchess of Kent, photographed in Lausanne with Queen Fredericka of Greece in 1949, is uncharacteristically wearing a simple cotton dress. She took to wearing cotton dresses to support the floundering Lancashire cotton industry. Both women are wearing ultra-fashionable white peep-toe sandals.

Left: The Duke and Duchess of Kent remain chic even in the country, photographed here in 1934.

As I saw them

By Lady Diana Cooper

May 10, 1959

In June King Edward VIII invited us to cruise in a yacht he had chartered in the Mediterranean. Greatly excited and flattered, we joined The Nahlin on the Dalmatian coast. From Split I wrote to Conrad:

We went aboard the Nahlin and there were greeted by the young King, radiant in health, wearing spick-and-span little shorts, straw sandals and two crucifixes on a chain round his neck. Our fellow guests are Helen Fitzgerald, Pootz,

and Humphrey Butler, Jack Aird and Wallis.

We set steam for a near island. No sooner was the yacht sighted than the whole village turned out – a million children and gay

folk smiling and cheering. Half of them didn't know which the King was and must have been surprised when they were told. He had no hat (the child's hair gleaming), espadrilles, the same little shorts and a tiny blue-and-white singlet bought in one of their own villages.

The other girls were rather seriously fixed, but Duff and I followed our sovereign's lead. I sported the old green zipped trousers, striped shirt and a straw hat bought at Le Puy last week. Duff wore navy shorts, too loose and sagging below his reduced tummy, the white sandals that we bought at Verona together, and the old blue-and-white top. The rather battered yachting cap (battered by my packing, not by wear) gave him a W.W. Jacobs bos'n look.

To go back to yesterday, no sooner had we anchored than the King got into a row-boat and went off to discover a sandy beach, rowing through all the craft and canoes and top-heavy tourist-launches and the rubbernecks glaring at the decks of the Nahlin – and not knowing that they were seeing what they were looking for.

After some bathing and some sleeping and some gossiping and a cup of tea, we boarded the royal launch respectably dressed (by that I mean trousers for the men only, no hats, but sweaters, no naked torsos showing).

There's no traffic in Ragusa and there are baroque and gothic churches and palaces and monasteries. The people were mostly in national dress and on this occasion, they were all out in orderly rows, both sides of the streets that the consul had mapped out for our tour of the sights. They were cheering their lungs out with looks of ecstasy on their faces.

The King walks a little ahead talking to the consul or mayor, and we follow adoring it. He waves his hand, half-saluting. He is utterly himself and unselfconscious. That, I think, is the reason why he does some things (that he likes) superlatively well. He does not *act*.

In the middle of the procession he stopped for a good two minutes to tie up his shoe. There was a knot, and it took time. We were all left staring at his behind. You or I would have risen above the lace, wouldn't we, until the procession was over?

But it did not occur to him to wait, and so the people said: "Isn't he human! Isn't he natural! He stopped to do up his shoe like any of us!"

After sightseeing, drinks in a hotel garden. The King makes the cocktails himself for Helen and Pootz, Duff and the staff have beer, I have white wine of the country, Wallis has whisky and water. The staff say that they hate the King to see the consuls the first day because they are always in such a trance of ecstasy and nerves that all the plans the King makes with them are forgotten as soon as they are out of the presence.

King Edward VIII relaxes on a cruise of the Adriatic with his 'friend' Wallis Simpson and Mrs Herman Rogers. Mrs Simpson, clutching a pair of sunglasses, still looks neat as a pin.

The style icon endures

Above: On a tour of Canada in 1919 Edward, Prince of Wales leapt on to a horse in his Savile Row suit.

Right: The Duke and Duchess of Windsor lounge in the garden of Government House in the Bahamas circa 1942. The Duke was Governor during World War II from 1940-1945. He is wearing a comfortable cotton suit, while the Duchess is in a beautifully co-ordinated blue, red and white shirtwaister with a red belt and statement jewellery.

Country casuals

By Anna Murphy   *September 14, 2022*

Away from the public eye the Queen didn't need any help getting dressed. She wore clothes that didn't get in the way of walking and riding, dogs and horses: tweed skirts, lace-up brown shoes, sensible woollies, a headscarf, assorted raincoats.

The colours she chose were those of our country, her country: earth, moss, heather, lichen. She wore a kind of camouflage. In her private life she could, at last, blend in.

The 81-year-old
Prince Philip, Duke
of Edinburgh, takes
the reins in a carriage
driving competition
at the Royal Windsor
Horse Show in 2002,
a year before he
retired from the sport.
Regulations demand
the wearing of a
country tweed jacket,
rug, hat, gloves and
whip. The jacket does
not fit Prince Philip as
perfectly as his clothes
usually do, but he
famously did not like
to part with clothes so
perhaps he had merely
lost some weight.

Princess Elizabeth and the Duke of Edinburgh walk the grounds of Broadlands (home of the Mountbattens) on their honeymoon in 1947. Both are still formally dressed in suits and the princess is wearing Queen Victoria's massive sapphire brooch, which Prince Albert gifted to Victoria for their wedding.

Diana's black sheep jumper goes on sale at Sotheby's

By George Willoughby

June 27, 2023

A red and white "black sheep" jumper worn by Diana, Princess of Wales, is expected to fetch up to £70,000 at Sotheby's in New York later this year.

Diana first wore the jumper to watch Charles, at the time her fiancé, in a polo match in June 1981. It was designed by Sally Muir and Joanna Osborne for their label Warm & Wonderful.

The designers said: "The first we knew of Lady Diana Spencer wearing the sweater was when we saw her on the front page of a Sunday newspaper. Her influence was impactful almost immediately, leading to a surge in sales and public awareness of our small label, for which we will be forever grateful."

A few weeks later, Muir and Osborne made a new sweater for the princess after Buckingham Palace told them it had been damaged. For decades it was not known what had happened to the original, but this year it was found in a box in the designers' attic. Warm & Wonderful stopped producing the black sheep style in 1994, but it was reissued in 2020 as a collaboration with the Rowing Blazers brand.

Sotheby's is offering the original sweater as part of its "Fashion Icons" sale, held during New York Fashion Week from August 31 to September 13.

In January, the auction house set a new record for the most valuable Diana dress to have been sold when an aubergine ballgown fetched £474,870. Cynthia Houlton, global head of fashion and accessories at Sotheby's, said the jumper "carries the whispers of Princess Diana's grace, charm and eye for fashion".

Lady Diana Spencer at Windsor Polo in June 1981, in jeans, a frilly pie-crust collar shirt, part of the Sloane Ranger uniform, and the infamous "black sheep" jumper.

A month before her wedding
Lady Diana Spencer again
watches Prince Charles play
polo, this time in a lace-
collared floral print blouse
and a pair of dungarees.

Prince Charles in breeks looks quite the old-fashioned country gent, but his fiancée, Lady Diana Spencer, injects some colour into the Balmoral countryside in a Peruvian alpaca knit. She bought the sweater on February 8, 1981, from a Peruvian shop in London, her engagement to Prince Charles was announced 16 days later. After these images were published in May, the shop sold 400 copies of this sweater design.

Polo playing is a tradition in the royal family and Prince Charles, now Charles III, began playing at the age of 15, retiring from the game aged 57. On the polo field he cut rather a dashing figure, perhaps because here, if nowhere else, he could legitimately look dishevelled after a few chukkas. It must have been liberating.

Left: Prince Charles at full throttle at Oak Brook Polo Club in Chicago 1986.

Above: A post-match celebration at Cowdray Park Polo Club in 1981.

Fit for a queen

By Michael Roberts

June 28, 1981

It was a very tight squeeze at Rigby and Peller, the Queen's corsetières, last week, as many frail, genteel country ladies negotiated the narrow stairway leading to the tiny first-floor Mayfair salon to await their swimming-costume fittings amid boxes of Lycra stays.

In the workroom, a formidable black one-piece was being whisked away into a box for a countess. Meanwhile a rather racy black-and-red floral print bikini was being secretly swathed in tissue "for the Duchess of Kent".

Did anyone anticipate a trousseau-time visit from Lady Diana Spencer? The ladylike staff twinkled with hope. If honeymoon-bound Lady Diana does indeed favour Rigby and Peller with her heroic bosom, she will be joining Her Majesty, Princess Margaret, several other

The sun-worshipping Princess Margaret is photographed on the beach in Mustique in 1976.

relatives, Barbara Cartland, and a few thousand Miss Marple look-alikes, whose cantilevered figures owe everything to the delicate skills of the royal (by appointment since 1960) corsetières.

We hope, however, she won't be as picky as Margaret, who always insists on the stiffly-boned" Lollobrigida Look for her frequent sojourns in Mustique. "I don't particularly like it," shrugs Mrs Tessa Seiden, who has run the business for the past 25 years, but she insists "that regal 'hourglass' effect is achieved with a 'guipure.'"

The business of royal corsetry naturally means that Mrs Seiden, a Hungarian émigrée, has to be utterly, utterly discreet. After all, intimate info concerning royal underpinnings is hardly the sort of thing to be blithely bandied about. However, it would be giving nothing away to say that they specialise in "The Fuller Figure".

"When people first come here I say straight away, 'what is your problem?' because – let's face it – they wouldn't be

here if they didn't have one," says Mrs Seiden emphatically.

Thus there is much concern with "balancing" the ladies' stately figures with "bones" (not whalebones anymore, but flexible steel rods) and with uplifting wires. "Girls are definitely getting bigger and bigger," muses Mrs Seiden. "It must be the pill."

Mrs Seiden's "girls" generally hover around the 50-ish mark. "That generation appreciates the workmanship," she explains: "A customer came in recently with a costume she bought nine years ago. We altered it and I said: 'See you again in another nine years.'" At Rigby and Peller, June and July are the busy months for custom-built costumes, but customers buy in bulk in the winter months "for their world cruises". "And we sell up to a size 52," cries Mrs Seiden, suddenly whipping out a nifty floral wigwam.

As the phone buzzes with clients desperate for new corsets, bust bodices (bras) and foundation garments (this year beige is in, pink is out) she takes time off to peruse

her royal warrant. "A friend said it was awarded for giving the Queen such wonderful support. In the early days I was told to go to the Palace wearing a black dress and a hat," she says, chortling at the incongruity of herself dressed and Her Majesty not. Is she ever tempted to discuss The Royal Figure? "Never!" says Mrs Seiden firmly.

Above: Princess Margaret, seen here in 1960, and her big sister were the last of a generation of hat wearers. A clear signal that they were off duty was the wearing of a headscarf.

Right: Princess Margaret looks incredibly chic in Tanganyika, October, 1956.

Above: Princess Diana looked very much at ease on the ski slopes, eventually opting for strong shapes in bold colours, seen here at Lech, Austria, in 1994.

Right: Diana Princess of Wales shows that you can't go wrong if you keep things simple and the pie crust collars were a distant memory. At Wimbledon in 1994 she enjoys the tennis in a red, sleeveless belted dress with gold buttons and gold jewellery. She is with Princess Michael of Kent.

The Duchess of Cornwall, now Queen Camilla, looks at her happiest and most relaxed at the races. This is a style of dressing she understands and is comfortable with and it shows. At the first day of Royal Ascot in 2006 (right), enjoying the company of a dapper Prince Philip in top hat and tails, the Duchess wears a sartorial cocktail of gold and cream. On Day Two of Royal Ascot in 2013 (left) the Duchess in a soft sea-green silk coat and wearing Princess Alexandra's Prince of Wales brooch with emerald drop, looks exuberantly elegant.

Nice and easy does it

Far left: The Duchess of Sussex attends the Invictus Games in Netherlands in 2022 wearing a navy Celine jacket with gold buttons, rolled up Moussy jeans and a white shirt.

Left: A simple wicker clutch from J Crew, a pair of Tom Ford aviator sunglasses and a sleeveless denim Carolina Herrera dress, the Duchess of Sussex is effortlessly stylish attending the polo in July 2018.

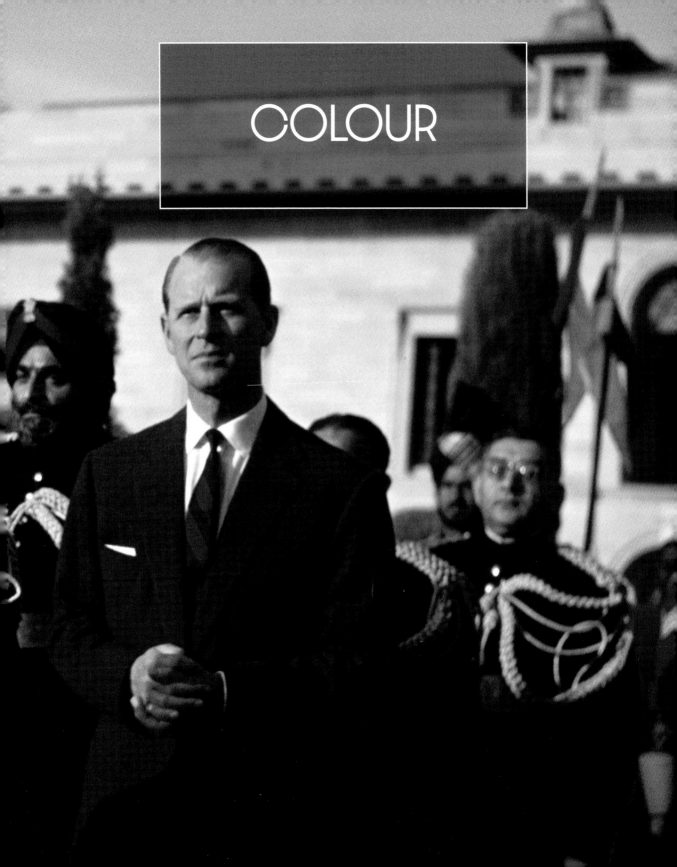

COLOUR

Queen Elizabeth II is so commonly associated with the wearing of colour that it is easy to overlook that in regal terms she was being quite radical. Her attitude was "I have to be seen to be believed", so she had to stand out from the crowd. Being only 5ft 3in, and even smaller as she aged, Her Majesty could have been easy to miss, but as a top-to-toe vision in buttercup yellow, cobalt blue, emerald green, turquoise or scarlet, the Queen was seen. Mission accomplished.

Historically the royals wore principally silver and gold to emphasise their royal status, though flashes of colour were acceptable. After the death of Prince Albert in 1861, Queen Victoria wore widow's weeds until her own demise in 1901. Widows traditionally were required to wear black for two years and then move into half-mourning, wearing grey, purple or white, for a further period. Victoria turned mourning into a national fetish and became the embodiment of grief, favouring black for over half of her reign. Her Court was expected to follow suit. Virtually retiring from public life, she was widely criticised for being more widow than monarch.

Thanks to Queen Victoria manufacturers and purveyors of mourning clothes flourished. The London General Mourning Warehouse in Regent Street did a roaring trade supplying everything funereal – dresses, hats, shawls, veils, shoes, gloves and jewellery (only jet was acceptable). The Queen was reputed to be a customer. Despite the familiarity of her outfits, she apparently did not like to wear the same dress twice.

Princess Alexandra was hampered in her choice of colour by her mother-in-law's obsession with mourning. She opted to wear white instead, until the old Queen's death, after which she favoured lavender and grey, as well as the traditional silver and gold. Slim into old age, she also wore dark, beautifully tailored suits.

The fashionable Princess Mary, wife of Prince George, later George V, was constrained by her husband's conservative taste and his dogged attachment to tradition. Diarist Chips Cannon described Queen Mary as "regally majestic", "looking like the Jungfrau, white and sparkling in the sun" and formidable in appearance "like talking to St Paul's Cathedral". She also favoured gold and silver for formal occasions and adopted a subdued palette of lavender and shades of grey.

A stickler for standards of dress, George V was heavily critical of his son, Edward, Prince of Wales, later briefly Edward VIII, who was passionate about his clothes and imbued the royal dress with more than a dash of flamboyance . He was a connoisseur of colour, with one of his more memorable suits being lime green with a violet check. He introduced the midnight-blue evening suit as an alternative to black because it photographed better, and favoured boldly coloured ties and pocket squares. He also inspired fashionable demand for loud Fair Isle slipover vests.

The stylish Princess Marina actually had a colour named for her, "Marina blue", after a dress she wore to Royal Ascot created a sensation. Princess Diana on the other hand was criticised by the French press for wearing clothes the colours of "boiled sweets".

Colour sends out subliminal messages, it can be used as a silent tribute or compliment when making state visits. One of the most famous examples is an ivory and emerald-green duchesse-satin evening dress by Norman Hartnell that Queen Elizabeth II wore to Pakistan in 1961. It was the first visit since Pakistan had won independence and the sculptural frock combined the country's national colours in a complimentary sartorial salute.

Whether by design or accident, Catherine, Princess of Wales, sends subliminal patriotic messages when she opts for one-colour ensembles in red, white or blue, subtly reflecting the colours of the Union Jack.

Left: Princess Charlotte Augusta, the only child of King George IV and Caroline the Queen Consort is dressed a la mode in the best Regency style. This portrait of her by George Dawe is dated circa 1817, the year of her death during childbirth.

Above: Caroline of Brunswick (1768-1821), wife of Prince George, later King George IV and Queen Consort of Britain, is seen here in a painting by Sir Thomas Lawrence. When she married the Prince of Wales in 1795 he had already been married a year earlier, illegally, to Maria Fitzherbert and he was determined not to like the bride selected for him. Caroline was generally regarded as being rather good looking, though lacking in decorum. She liked George no better than he liked her. She was libelled and abused throughout her life, not least by her husband who tried to divorce her, barred her from his coronation (she turned up and was stopped by bayonets at the door of the Abbey) and who did not have the common humanity to inform her when their only daughter died. The public liked her and perhaps in this portrait, in her sumptuous red velvet dress, she reveals her determination to be neither cowed nor subjugated.

Diamonds
are forever

Queen Victoria may have worn widow's weeds for 40 years, but she was certainly not dull. The clothes may have been exclusively black, but they were liberally dotted with braid, fringing, and lace, family orders on her left shoulder, jewellery, jewellery and yet more jewellery. She is wearing the small, lightweight diamond crown she commissioned for comfort, the diamond collet necklace, earrings and bar brooch as well as numerous rings and bracelets.

Jane Eastoe

Power of the palette

By Anna Murphy

September 14, 2022

"If I wore beige," the Queen once said, "nobody would know who I am." Dress head to toe in cerise or turquoise, on the other hand, and there was no question who One might be, no difficulty picking One out in a crowd. At heart Her Majesty's choices were the regal equivalent of the hi-vis jacket, and often almost as bright.

Queen Elizabeth II steps out in a bold floral-print silk dress in shades of pink, green and gold. Her statement hat is a positive bouquet of pink and gold flowers, complete with a veil. The look is completed with white gloves and handbag, pearls and the Duchess of Teck's corsage brooch.

Left: By 1966 Queen Elizabeth was beginning to slim down her fashion silhouette with neatly tailored dresses. On a tour of the West Indies in 1966 she wears a boldly-printed orange and gold dress and short collarless jacket. The Launer handbag is cream, the shoes cream and gold, the gloves white and the joyous hat an explosion of fabric loops that correspond precisely to the colours of the dress, with the odd hint of green thrown in for good measure.

Above: Queen Elizabeth wears a finely-pleated, dark green chiffon dress during her tour of Australia in March 1954. She combines this elegantly with a white hat, gloves and bag, with pearls around her neck, and the Duchess of Teck's pearl and diamond earrings.

Above: Queen Elizabeth II wears a chic yellow silk dress and flowerpot hat in Ghana, November 1960.

Below: On a tour of India in 1961 Queen Elizabeth wears a pale pink dress with a pretty self-fabric spot pattern. Her small hat is a cascade of pink petals while the remaining accessories are white.

Queen Elizabeth wraps up
warmly in a bright green,
soft-wool coat and dress on
a visit to Lancashire in May
2006. The matching felt hat is
trimmed in black.

Queen Elizabeth pulled out all the stops on a visit to France in 2014 for the 70th anniversary commemorations of the D-Day Landings in Normandy. She wore a baby-pink collarless coat in a Chanel-type tweed, with matching hat. Her Majesty wore pearls and a flower brooch displaying the Williamson 23.6 carat pink diamond at its heart. The stone was a wedding present and a brooch was constructed around it in 1953, along with 203 white diamonds to further enhance it.

In mourning and in white

By Hannah Betts   *July 23, 2005*

In 1938 Queen Elizabeth's white wardrobe wowed Paris.

Ask any girl what draws her to the idea of playing princesses and the answer comes back at once: the clothes. It is thus a source of constant feminine frustration that the present British monarchy botches this aspect so royally.

Never was this more apparent than in the fact that a woman who favoured Peter Pan collars, meringue evening wear and a heavy fringe flick became its fashion icon.

The distrust of fashion stems from the clan's matriarch, Queen Elizabeth the Queen Mother, for whom it invoked the spectre of "that woman", the fashion plate Wallis Simpson. Each of the Windsor offspring hatched her own look: for the heir, Queen Elizabeth, it was the high collared formality of her coronation; for the spare, Margaret Rose, a let-it-all-hang-out kaftan.

But at some time in the post-Jubilee period, the styles of these women fused, and the Queen Mother and her daughters began to affect a collective mumsiness: platform shoes, WI hats and a penchant for periwinkle blue. Not even the excuse of having to buy British could account for such a stalwart pursuit of dowdiness. Even the Duchess of Cornwall shines by comparison.

It is curious, then, that this summer Buckingham Palace is asking the public to accept the image of the dear old Queen Mum as style icon. Buckingham Palace's exhibition of Queen Elizabeth's "white wardrobe" centres on the outfits created by Norman Hartnell for the state visit to France in 1938, a mission intended to strengthen the *entente cordiale*.

The abdication crisis was a recent wound, war a gathering menace. Five days before their departure,

the Queen's mother, the Countess of Strathmore, died. Hartnell was given three weeks to transform his collection into something befitting a monarch in mourning. Black was deemed inappropriate for the Parisian summer, and so he resolved upon white. The Queen left Buckingham Palace in shades of jet, but she arrived in Paris an image of innocence, and a wave of prewar romanticism was born.

The exhibition will feature eight frocks, six of which were worn in Paris, including two examples of the visit's signature look, the crinoline. This cultivated anachronism, with its exaggerated feminine silhouette, marked a radical departure from the figure-hugging bias-cuts of the

Queen Elizabeth dressed in white from top-to-toe for her visit to France in July 1938, seen here at Le Parc de Bagatelle.

1930s. The mood was fantastical: baroquely elaborate confections ornamented with diamante, sequins, spangles and silver thread.

Hartnell, the first couturier knight, described simplicity as "the death of the soul", and the aesthetic, here at least, is irredeemably chocolate-box Victoriana. These days, crinoline ladies crop up in the most ignominious of places: on sanitary towel disposal bags or lavatory roll shields. But the response at the time was rapturous, at home and abroad.

According to the curator, Caroline de Guitaut, there were no negative responses, even among Parisians, accustomed to thumbing their noses at British style. *Vogue* immediately devoted an issue to royal dressing and the Queen's

Scottish heritage, while Schiaparelli and Molyneux included tartan in their next collections. Years later, Christian Dior was still extolling the white wardrobe's virtues. Even the Germans were forced to acknowledge the Palace's prowess at public relations.

For the new Queen it was a personal and political coup. As a woman, she had styled her rather matronly body to good effect. Politically, she had created an image that Britain, and the world, could mass behind. As de Guitaut explains: "The footage reveals amazing scenes in Paris. There was a *fête champêtre* atmosphere, with performers appearing at a garden party dancing on floating islands in an extraordinarily fey kind of way. It was a fairytale." And Elizabeth was its fairy queen.

The costume historian CW Cunnington remarked: "Never has fashion been more ironic than in this attempt to revive, for an evening dress, the modes current on the eve of the Franco-Prussian War."

Ironic it may have been, and more than a little naff perhaps, but the white wardrobe is further evidence that the Queen Mother was a canny old bird, even as a fledgeling queen. She may have been a greater admirer of nags than frocks, but she knew how iconography works: when reality is too nightmarish, monarchy transforms itself into a dream. Hartnell's next job would be creating uniforms; the Queen's reaching a point where she could look the East End in the face. But, for the summer of 1938, the image was all lace and tulle.

Queen Elizabeth in a Hartnell French lace dress with George VI, in the uniform of Admiral of the Fleet, at a reception at City Hall in Paris in July, 1938. In 1951 Christian Dior commented: "whenever I try to think of something particularly beautiful, I always think of those lovely dresses that Mr Hartnell made for your beautiful Queen when she visited Paris."

The perfectly proper princess

From our correspondent *August 7, 1962*

Thousands of excited, calypso-singing Jamaicans danced through the streets here into the early hours of this morning celebrating their first day of independence. The Commonwealth's newest member became independent at midnight, when her black, gold and green flag was flown for the first time. Princess Margaret and Lord Snowdon headed a vast audience in the national stadium as the Union Jack was hauled down, ending 307 years of British rule, and the new flag run up. Bells pealed in all the churches and schools in the 4,000 villages of Jamaica, and beacons and bonfires blazed from hill and mountain top. Fireworks lit up the sky and ships' sirens blared.

The Princess in a bouffant white evening gown with a bell-shaped skirt and a diamond tiara, sat beside her husband and the island's first Governor-General, Sir Kenneth Blackburne. She was greeted by the Prime Minister, Sir Alexander Bustamante.

In his first official act as Prime Minister of Independent Jamaica, Sir Alexander Bustamante [later] presented Princess Margaret with a dinner service of elegantly designed Jamaican pottery on behalf of his Government and people. With the dinner service were five baskets of seashells. At the ceremony, the Princess, accompanied by her husband, wore a dress of pink and tangerine printed chiffon with flying panels and a coolie hat of tangerine silk petals. A message from U Thant, acting Secretary-General of the United Nations, through Dr. Ralph Bunche, who was representing him, said: "Jamaica has provided a striking example of the principle of self-determination which is the fundamental objective of the United Nations for all non-self-governing peoples. You may be sure of a cordial welcome to the world community of nations by members of the United Nations."

A glowing vision in a yellow-gold pin-tucked silk dress, Princess Margaret boldly accessorises it with a wondrous frou-frou of a tulle hat, pearls, gloves and a pale pink handbag.

Bold, brave and bright

Left: In July 1997 the Princess of Wales visited Harrow in a belted shift dress by Catherine Walker.

Right: Diana, Princess of Wales, embraces colour-blocking on a trip to Hong Kong in 1989 in this Catherine Walker ensemble. Red, violet and pale yellow, who knew that would work?

Bananas? Regal duchess needs tips from Victoria

By Hilary Rose   *April 19, 2014*

The Duchess of Cambridge has pulled off another fashion coup and, with her choice of overwhelmingly British designers, given a boost to British fashion.

On tour in Australia and New Zealand, her wardrobe has been a regal roll call of some of the best designers in the world, many of whom call London home.

"The Duchess of Cambridge's support for British fashion makes her a global ambassador for the industry," said the London-based designer Emilia Wickstead. The Duchess wore an aquamarine coat dress by Wickstead for the couple's trip to Dunedin, on New Zealand's South Island. "The value of this is immeasurable. She has instigated a sophisticated shift towards dressing up which translates into a fresh approach to dressing a young generation."

Fashion commentators have noticed a definite shift in style and with her bold, British choices, the Duchess has projected a demure, mature and ladylike image. "She's definitely adopted a more regal style, and she's choosing more British designers, which is great news for the British fashion industry," said Jane Bruton, editor of *Grazia* magazine. "The turning point for me was that yellow Roksanda Ilincic dress, which Prince William said made her look like a banana. That was when I thought she's really developing a style of her own."

Justine Picardie, editor in chief of UK *Harper's Bazaar* agrees: "On this tour she's making strong, confident choices about what to wear, without ever looking like a fashion victim. It's also interesting to see how her outfits – the bold, block colours – are suggestive of the Queen's wardrobe, and I mean that as a compliment. I let out a cheer when I saw her in the yellow Roksanda Ilincic dress – not only because she looked amazing, but because it was such a tremendous endorsement of British fashion."

The Ilincic dress she wore on arrival in Sydney is a perfect example of the duchess's new, tailored – and expensive – style. Hem lengths are longer, which is both fashionable and more demure than some of the thigh-skimming frocks she has worn in the past. There have been sharply fitted coat dresses, practical and beautiful, from Catherine Walker, McQueen and Erdem.

Don't be fooled, though, by the thrifty-chic high street princess schtick, which is starting to wear a bit thin: those Zara jackets and LK Bennett dresses fit her so perfectly because she has set the seamstresses at Buckingham Palace to work on them. By the time they have finished, that £150 dress is halfway to becoming couture.

It seems likely that, as is rumoured, the Queen had a quiet word and told her to aim for something more regal than Reiss for this all-important tour. And while this has prompted many in the fashion pack to remark that Kate dresses like a 52-year-old and that most of her clothes could just as easily be worn by the Duchess of Cornwall – which they could – others point out that she isn't just any 32-year-old and shouldn't dress like one.

Right: The Duchess of Cambridge presents the trophy at Wimbledon, July 2022, in a canary-yellow Roksanda dress.

Above: The Duchess of Cambridge wears a white Alexander McQueen coat dress at the Menin Gate in Belgium, 2017, also worn for Princess Charlotte's christening in 2015.

While few would disagree that the Duchess has managed with aplomb the transition from pretty Berkshire girl next door to glamorous consort, fashion insiders argue that she could do even better with help from an industry pro. Diana, Princess of Wales, didn't have a natural fashion instinct either, but she recruited an editor from *Vogue* to help her find her style. As far as we know, the only advice Kate has sought has been from Angela Kelly, the Queen's senior dresser. How about Victoria Beckham? There's a woman who has her finger on the fashion pulse. Like Kate, she does things her way, she loves a stiletto, and she knows better than Kate what works for the camera. And she knows how to dress a skinny brunette.

Previous pages: The Duchess of Cambridge wears a red coat by Catherine Walker at a welcoming ceremony in New Zealand in April 2014, and a svelte blue dress by Jenny Packham in October 2018.

Left: The Duchess of Cambridge wears a baby-blue coat dress by Emilia Wickstead on a trip to Luxembourg in May 2017.

Right: The Princess of Wales attends Royal Ascot in June 2023 wearing a red Alexander McQueen dress with a Philip Treacy hat.

Thoroughly modern Meghan

By Harriet Walker

December 21, 2022

Not all superheroes wear capes, they say, but the Duchess of Sussex chose one by Stella McCartney for the Queen's funeral in September. It was part old Hollywood, part mafioso widow, topped off with a tilted Dior hat made by the British milliner Stephen Jones that used minimalist design to maximum effect. Not only did she stand miles apart, sartorially speaking, from the rest of The Firm in their fusty coat dresses, she had a nation furiously googling "opera gloves" on what was supposed to be a day of quiet contemplation.

Above: A pregnant Duchess of Sussex looks exquisite in a clean-lined matching coat and dress with black and iron-grey sequinned motifs, by the Canadian designer Erdem on a visit to Canada House in March 2019.

Right: the Duchess concludes her last official royal duty in a green silk Emilia Wickstead caped dress with matching hat by milliner William Chambers.

The newly-engaged Meghan Markle wears Givenchy on her first official visit in June 2018. She accompanied Queen Elizabeth II to the opening of the Mersey Gateway Bridge in Widnes. The cream dress was mid-calf in length with a short cape covering the shoulders and upper arms in a masterly display of pared-back elegance.

Left: The royals use colour to pay an unspoken compliment to their hosts on foreign visits. For the Queen's visit to Pakistan in 1961 Norman Hartnell utilised the colours of the flag in a sculptural silk-satin dress.

Above: In 2019 the Duchess of Cambridge politely covers up in a stand-out dark-green sequinned dress that won style plaudits.

FINAL
FLOURISHES

No one could rival Queen Elizabeth II for her devotion to a full complement of artfully coordinated accessories. She was rarely seen "on duty" without a hat, gloves, handbag, sensible shoes and fine jewellery, which she described as her "best bits".

Milliners in particular are grateful for such high-profile patronage. "I design for royalty throughout the world because royals actually wear hats," milliner Philip Treacy observed. "They are the true hat-wearers of the twenty-first century, the ultimate influencers who keep the millinery business going."

The Irishman once asked Her Majesty if she enjoyed wearing a hat. "They're part of the uniform," she replied.

The hat had to match the outfit, show her face and allow her to easily climb in and out of the limousine. She received heavy press criticism for a jaunty peaked cap she wore on a visit to San Diego in 1983. Couturier Hardy Amies later apologised for this apparent aberration but his client is said to have commented that she could not see what was wrong with it.

While Elizabeth II happily changed her styles of headwear, her grandmother, Queen Mary, favoured only what were referred to as "terrifying toques" throughout her life. Queen Elizabeth, the Queen Mother, resolutely sported confections smothered in feathery blooms and veiling for over 50 years. She appeared soft and fluffy, but behind her cultivated sweetness of appearance she was regarded as "a steel hand in a velvet glove".

Royal patronage sets shop tills ringing. When the Duchess of Cambridge stepped out in a pair of £185 LK Bennett nude shoes she caused a retail frenzy. According to Hilary Rose in *The Times*, the fashion chain sold out as fast as it could stock them. Brands from Jimmy Choo to Next added their versions. Marks & Spencer reportedly sold a pair of its £19.50 nude courts every two minutes thanks to the Kate effect.

Sales of handbags made by Launer, Queen Elizabeth II's favourite supplier, rose by 52% in 2013, after the monarch carried one to Prince William's wedding in 2012. Reportedly at least one new style was purchased by the Queen each year, the handles made longer than usual so that it could be carried in the crook of the royal arm.

Copying the royal family's jewellery presents more of a challenge. Queen Victoria not only inherited many priceless pieces, but she also treated herself to new trinkets, spending about £185,000 on jewellery and silver at Garrard in her lifetime (equating to around £17.5 million today). Additionally she acquired enviable jewels in the form of "gifts" from India, brought back by the Prince of Wales after his visit in 1875.

As the twentieth century began, Queen Alexandra draped herself in jewellery day and night in an exhibition of queenly magnificence. Though her dresses were comparatively plain, the overall effect when the jewellery was piled on, to modern eyes, is pure costume drama.

Queen Mary, with a reputation of a magpie, had an eye for a good jewel and added considerably to the royal collection. She could be unscrupulous. On the death of her sister, Empress Marie Feodorovna, she "purchased" some of the best pieces from the Romanov casket, offering half their value, but never actually paid her debt. Her granddaughter Elizabeth II finally repaid what was owed in 1968. After all, she had inherited them all.

The late monarch may turn out to be the last to pile on the bling, sporting matching tiara, necklace, earrings, brooch and bracelet with aplomb on state occasions. No wonder she thought of them as "my best bits".

Today's younger royals adopt a more pared-down approach. Perhaps you have to gradually acquire the confidence to carry off millions of pounds' worth of jewellery worn all at once, or perhaps such full-on displays of ostentatious wealth are today regarded as insensitive.

This pair of silk-satin side lacing boots were made for Queen Victoria by the shoemaker Gundry & Sons. The inners are made of soft and pliable leather. The boots are a petite size four and reveal Her Majesty's fondness for soft pastel colours before she took to wearing exclusively black. The boots are in the Royal Collection and when acquired were showing serious signs of wear and tear with rips in the fabric. Extensive conservation work was undertaken to restore the boots to their former sumptuous glory.

This straw bonnet, lined with organza and tied with a black silk ribbon, was made for the Queen by royal hatter Robert Heath Ltd. This practical hat is a world away from the heavy Victorian bonnets more normally associated with her.

The royal hunt of the jewels

Fascinated by the royal family's dynasty of gems, *The Times* fashion editor Suzy Menkes embarked on a long odyssey to discover their history.

By Suzy Menkes   *November 18, 1985*

The most fabulous collection of jewels in the modern world is worn by the British royal family. Yet the glittering gems are the most private and personal part of our royal heritage.

I started to research the royal jewels with a fashion editor's instinct that gems not only suggest opulence and majesty but also reveal the character and personality of their owners. My detective work, over three years and across three continents, led to a book, *The Royal Jewels*. With official help I learnt the major pieces in the Queen's collection and recognised them like favourite children. There was Queen Victoria's sapphire brooch, given to her by Albert on their wedding day. From Victoria, too, came the Jubilee necklace with a monumental pearl and diamond crown as its centrepiece.

I discovered that the Queen's familiar circle tiara, hung like a mobile with lustrous pearls, was once the property of the exotic Russian Grand-Duchess Vladimir. With the help of William Summers of Garrard, the Crown Jewellers, I traced Princess Diana's bow knot tiara with its bobbing pearls back to Queen Mary and the First World War.

I was curious, not about what I was told, but about what I observed – the diplomatic silence on the subject of Indian jewels; the confusion surrounding Queen Mary's overwhelming acquisitions; the apparent lack of any official list of which jewels were Crown property and which were personal gems; the frozen response to the name of the Duchess of Windsor. The photographic archives at Windsor and the library at *The Times* yielded revelations – the Queen Mother's favourite necklace of looped diamonds and pearls was around Princess Alexandra's neck on her wedding day: "Granny's tiara" and the same drop pearl brooch appeared on both Queen Mary and the Queen.

This portrait of Queen Victoria, by Franz Xaver Winterhalter, was painted in 1859. Her Majesty wears the Diamond Diadem, with diamond earrings and the diamond collet necklace that were made for her by the jewellers Garrard & Co a year earlier. The diamonds had been removed from a garter badge and ceremonial sword for this express purpose. The diadem was designed for George IV's Coronation, but after a last-minute change of heart he never wore it and the jewels in it were only hired for the occasion. Queen Victoria had it reset with pearls and diamonds from the royal collection and wore it for her Coronation in 1838.

Left: Queen Elizabeth wears the Russian Fringe Tiara which was made by Garrard & Co. This was presented to Queen Alexandra on the occasion of her Silver Anniversary on behalf of 365 peeresses. Queen Alexandra had indicated a preference that the tiara be in the shape of a Russian peasant headdress, having seen her sister, the Empress of Russia, wearing one.

Above: Queen Elizabeth wears Queen Mary's Girls of Great Britain and Ireland Tiara. It was given to Mary of Teck on the occasion of her wedding to Prince George, after a collection raised £5,000. On Princess Mary's instructions the surplus was given to widows and orphans of men lost in the sinking of HMS Victoria. The tiara was made by Garrard & Co and was known fondly by Queen Elizabeth as 'Granny's tiara'. Queen Elizabeth also wears the V-shape diamond and ruby bandeau collar, with drop diamond pendant, which was given to her by her parents on the occasion of her wedding in 1947. The ruby and diamond earrings were a gift from George V to Queen Mary on her 50th birthday.

The first delight was the discovery that the ledger of Queen Victoria's purchases at Garrard for her entire reign was crumbling in a cupboard at the Victoria and Albert Museum. The three months of lunch hours I spent decoding the salesmen's gothic gems. A torrent of jewels poured in from the Indian Empire and it is hard to trace the re-set gems.

At Cartier in Paris I found positive proof of one such transformation – an airy and elegant Edwardian diamond choker, culled from a massive Indian necklace in 1904. I believe that India was the inspiration for Queen Alexandra's opulent Edwardian style, and that the emeralds removed from that particular imperial tribute are the origin of the legend of the "Alexandra Emeralds".

Jewels that the Duchess of Windsor might have "got away with" is a subject that has obsessed the British public for 50 years. I searched for the mythical emeralds for three years through records in New Delhi, in the photographs of émigré and exiled Russians in France, Canada and America. I wept tears of frustration on a mean Paris street when I discovered that the Duchess

of Windsor's aged maid had died five days before our promised meeting. On the road to discovery I also dug up other stories and other emeralds. I sifted through 2,047 photographs of Queen Mary before I saw her wearing the globular cabochon platinum-set emeralds – proof that they were a wedding present from the Queen to her new daughter-in-law. That information was freely handed out by the Palace last week when Princess Diana chose to tie the necklace round her head.

Queen Mary's legendary appetite for gems had been fed by the Delhi durbar in 1911 but my efforts to trace the lustrous emeralds she received publicly from the ladies of India were frustrated by every source. The same was true of those other emeralds, the fiery green Cambridge gems that the Queen wears in her circle tiara in exchange for pearls. The family tale was that these exquisite emeralds – originally won in a German lottery – had been given away to his mistress by Queen Mary's feckless brother, Prince Frank of Teck. After another royal hunt for the jewels, I found out that the recipient was Lady Kilmorey, one of the "loose box" of

Edward VII's mistresses. Queen Mary bought her silence with one emerald brooch from the Cambridge suite. The lady who inherited it died in Ireland earlier this year.

Some of the jewels came with their own story line, trailing 1,000-year pedigrees. The mighty Koh-i-noor diamond bears a tale of greed, lust and conquest, and was nearly lost when a conquering British official left it in his tunic pocket and gave it to his servant to wash. A poignant episode in the *Royal Heritage* television film of 1969 shows the Queen caressing the carved Timur ruby, the "light of

---

The Cullinan V Heart Brooch is an 18.8 carat heart-shaped diamond and is pavé set with a border of smaller diamonds. It formed the centrepiece of a stomacher (a decorated panel which fills in the front of a woman's bodice), an item of jewellery Queen Mary was partial to. This came apart so that the pieces could be worn separately. The central stone was a cleaving from the famous Cullinan diamond, the largest rough diamond ever found. Queen Mary was gifted 102 cleavings from it in 1910.

the world", wishing that she could have a dress made in order to wear this piece of history. She never has.

The jewels that are not worn became as intriguing as the more public gems. I started to add up the tiaras and necklaces, the myriad brooches and jewels in the Queen's vast collection. I asked about the presentation gifts that occasionally surface as news or are even tinged with scandal. Royal family and household alike dropped an impenetrable glass screen.

I became interested in the modern jewellery designers whom the Prince of Wales has patronised and whether Princess Diana has added another charm to her bracelet. I also studied the origin of the Cullinan Diamond, which yielded the world's most impressive brooch. Our unostentatious Queen wore it with a corgi sitting on her lap. She calls it "Granny's chips".

Granny – the indomitable, majestic Queen Mary – is for me the most interesting character in the book. As a fashion editor I admire the taste and style the Duchess of Windsor brought to her fabulous collection of jewels. But the mystery, the intrigue and the potent power of jewels lies not in the "Alexandra emeralds", which I finally discovered were sold up by Queen Alexandra's daughter and bought as baubles by the Duke of Windsor for his wife. Queen Mary is the chief suspect in this entire royal detective story. She is the person who adored, acquired and categorised the jewels. She took the gems from her exiled Russian relatives, bought them at knock-down prices or, in the words of the witty diarist Sir Henry "Chips" Channon, "she bagged all the best".

Queen Mary, not the Duchess of Windsor, is at the glittering heart of the royal jewel collection. Hers was the passion, hers the pride, and hers the rivulets of diamonds to pass on to her granddaughter, the Queen.

Queen Mary magnificently decked out in opulent jewellery for the opening of her first parliament in 1911. She is wearing the Cullinan I (530.2 carats) and Cullinan II (317.4 carats) diamonds as a pendant brooch pinned to her garter sash. The Cullinan I, the world's largest cut diamond of any colour, is the large drop pendant which hangs from Cullinan II. In 1910, for George V's coronation, the stone was set at the top of the sovereign's sceptre, which had to be redesigned to accommodate it. The Cullinan diamonds are on show with the Crown Jewels at the Tower of London, except when in use.

The Fashion in Furs

From our correspondent   *November 1, 1922*

The habit of wearing fur has more in it than the mere desire for warmth. This was never more true than now, when fur is used, more often than not as an accessory and a trimming. Like beautiful jewels and old lace, it has the special quality of enhancing a woman's beauty to a high degree. The wearing of the skins of animals is, indeed, as ancient and primitive a custom as can be found. Perhaps it has partly survived to suggest the idea of every woman as Diana the Huntress.

On the practical side, it gives employment to thousands of people all over the world, and the obtaining of rare skins calls for high endurance of hardship on the part of the trapper. Like almost all good things, really fine fur is extremely expensive. One often wonders where are all those marvellously costly coats one sees in the saloons of the dressmaker. It is comparatively rare to see a whole cloak of chinchilla or sable on the shoulders of even a rich friend, and the stalls of a theatre often provide one with gloomy meditations on the unattractive appearance of shabby, dyed rabbit.

For while beautiful fur does add to the romance of woman's beauty, nothing so detracts from it as shabby fur.

H. R. H. PRINCESS MARY.

Princess Marina (**left**) in October 1946 and Princess Mary (**above**) in a white Arctic fox pelt circa 1913. There has been a change of approach, and in 2019 Queen Elizabeth II revealed that she no longer wore real fur.

To my Wallis from her David

By Suzy Menkes

March 14, 1987

Last week in Geneva, I held a piece of England's history in the palm of my hand. On one side of the gold compact was a crazy paving of rubies, sapphires and emeralds. On the other was engraved a map of the journeys that King Edward VIII took with Wallis Simpson. Inside lay a dusting of powder from the face of a woman for whom the King gave up his throne.

All the passion of that historic love affair is expressed in the Duchess of Windsor's jewels. They glow with vibrant colour, move with the body and are set with stones of sensual roundness. The animal magnetism that drew the unlikely couple together is reflected in their prowling panthers and exotic gem-set birds.

Today, some of the world's greatest private collectors are gathered in Palm Beach, Florida, one-time playground of the Duke and Duchess of Windsor. Inside a discreetly guarded mansion, specially selected guests will be allowed to finger and caress the gems, before they go on more public display, at Sotheby's New York next week. On April 2 and 3, these gifts of love – many with personal messages inscribed on the reverse, and some with royal ciphers – go under the hammer at Sotheby's Geneva. They are expected to raise £5 million for France's Institut Pasteur.

When I viewed the Duchess of Windsor's jewels, they were behind the pneumatically sealed double doors of Sotheby's new lakeside sales complex within the grand nineteenth-century Hotel Beau-Rivage. The white-walled stockroom was protected by bullet-proof glass doors, two security officers, and a Dobermann pinscher guard dog.

In a plain brown cardboard box lay the outstretched body of a diamond-encrusted panther. As I lapped the bracelet round my wrist, it seemed to spring to life, its mobile setting a superb piece of craftsmanship by Cartier in 1952.

Another panther with glittering yellow diamond eyes, sat coiled on a great ball of a sapphire clip; beside it, ready to leap from its emerald rock, was a rampant gold and enamel Great Cat.

Most fantastic of all was the flamingo brooch, an auctioneer's label tied round its spindly diamond-studded leg, below a plump breast and tactile jewelled tail feathers.

Completing the Windsor menagerie are crouching gem-set frogs and a delicate diamond butterfly, alighting on a succulent cabochon coral petalled with emeralds.

"Even without the royal connection, it is a unique collection," says Nicholas Rayner, chairman of Sotheby's Geneva, who will conduct the black-tie evening auction to be held in a marquee on the

lakeside to accommodate the 800 prospective clients.

"The duke was tremendously interested in design, style and fashion," says Nicholas Rayner. "He appreciated precious stones and workmanship. The duchess understood design and showmanship. The result is a continuity of style that is quite extraordinary." Mr Rayner showed me his favourite piece – the Van Cleef and Arpels bracelet, with its flexible diamond strap and a buckle of invisibly set sapphires. The duke gave it to Wallis on their wedding day and inscribed it *"For our contract 18-V-39"*.

Winking at me from inside its polythene bag was a fiery white-diamond ring, the size of a postage stamp, that the duke bought from New York jeweller Harry Winston. It is valued at £730,000 and called the "McLean diamond", after Washington collector Evalyn Walsh McLean. She bought the legendary Hope blue diamond – once worn by Louis XIV and by Queen Marie Antoinette and valued today at $20 million – and once claimed "when I neglect to wear jewels, it is a sign I'm becoming ill".

Of all the stones in the Wallis collection, the most superb is the translucent

emerald that the duchess described as her "engagement ring". It reportedly cost £10,000 when the King bought it from Cartier in October 1936. Britain was in the depths of the Depression and two weeks later he was vowing to help the poverty-stricken miners of South Wales.

The stone was cut from an emerald the size of a bird's egg belonging to an eighteenth-century Mogul emperor, according to a contemporary diarist Marie Belloc Lowndes, who had earlier dismissed Mrs Simpson's rocks as "dressmaker's emeralds".

It is easy to understand the scandal surrounding Mrs Simpson and her opulent

gifts from the new King – the jaunty tasselled necklace of faceted rubies made by Van Cleef for Wallis's 40th birthday in June 1936, or Cartier's twin ruby bracelet, that looked like a pair of opera glasses when the duchess was photographed wearing it by Cecil Beaton.

Sir Henry "Chips" Channon described the King's favourite as "literally smothered in rubies" at a dinner and "dripping with emeralds at the opera". How shocked he would have been to turn over the ruby necklace and read the words the King of England inscribed to another man's wife: *My Wallis from her David 19-VI-36*. That was in the summer of 1936 when the King's party left on a summer cruise and the couple were photographed in scanty beach clothes.

I picked up the bracelet of tiny, jewelled crosses and read, with a squirming sense of intrusion, the spidery inscriptions on the back. The earliest platinum cross reads "*We are too 25-X1-34*" in the same private language as the recently published Wallis and Edward Letters.

If the sensuous animals jewels are palpably gifts of love, the crosses on the duchess's bracelet are love letters. Each commemorates an eventful moment: "*God save the King for Wallis 16-VII-36*" says the sapphire cross bought after a pot shot was taken at Edward VIII. "*Wallis-David 23-6-35*" was for the Prince of Wales's birthday. The

amethyst cross is inscribed "*Appendectomy cross Wallis 31-VIII-44 David*".

Some of the jewels carry very private messages. "*Hold tight 27-111-34*" says the ruby and diamond bracelet the King gave Wallis after she had waved off to America the reigning royal favourite Lady Thelma Furness with the words: "Oh Thelma, the little man is going to be so lonely".

The twice-divorced duchess kept until her death her two previous wedding rings, inscribed with the respective husbands' initials and dates. They, and the tiny band of gold for which the King abdicated his crown, are valued at just £500.

Wallis may have been denied a royal title, but she became a queen of fashion.

The way she wore her showy jewels is shown in the archive pictures which face the photographs of jewels in Sotheby's lavish catalogue.

"This may not be the sale of the century in terms of value," says Nicholas Rayner, "but in every other single aspect it is the most important. The duke and duchess chose the jewels together and the whole collection is perfectly integrated. She didn't suddenly get attracted by antique jewels or by a futuristic piece. The style is extravagant, because they loved large and colourful pieces, but it is all in very good taste."

My favourite piece in the Windsor collection is the exotic jewelled flamingo. Like the duchess herself, it is frivolous, expensive, larger than life and fun.

Previous page: The Duke of Windsor bought his Duchess the ruby, sapphire and diamond flamingo brooch from Cartier as a gift in 1940 and it was one of her best known pieces. It was made from an existing necklace and four bracelets that the Duke of Windsor had broken up.

Left: Diarist Henry 'Chips' Cannon wrote of Wallis Simpson "Her collection of jewels is the talk of London." In a photograph entitled Jewels of the Globe, taken in 1936, Wallis wears on her wrist a delicate sapphire and diamond bracelet from Cartier from which hang tiny Latin crosses all bearing personal inscriptions. All bar one are set with sapphires, rubies, white and yellow diamonds, emeralds, aquamarines and amethysts. The first cross of platinum was given to her by the then Prince of Wales in 1934, though she did not have the final compliment of nine in this image. She wore it on the controversial Nahlin cruise with the then King in 1936. Edward VIII wore matching crosses on a chain around his neck. Wallis wears her emerald engagement ring and a sapphire and diamond bracelet, also from Cartier. On her head she wears a Van Cleef & Arpels asymmetrical hair ornament set with diamonds, a gift from Edward VIII.

No detail too small

A dandy of distinction, the Duke of Windsor's obsessive interest in his clothes extended, as one might expect, into his accessories. His shirts and ties were made for him by Hawes and Curtis in London's Jermyn Street, and he granted the company its first Royal Warrant in 1922.

Hawes and Curtis cut the duke's ties from a thicker than standard cloth and he favoured the four-in-hand tying style which produced a wide and elegant triangular knot. This was dubbed the Windsor knot and though the duke didn't invent this style of tying, he certainly popularised it. His equerry, Edward 'Fruity' Metcalf, also favoured this style of tie and he is thought to have first introduced the then Prince of Wales to it.

The Duke of Windsor used pocket squares to complement, not co-ordinate with, his ties, a sign of good taste and another ruse to introduce more colour and pattern into any outfit. After the deaths of the duke in 1972 and the duchess in 1986, his clothes were auctioned by Sotheby's in 1998. This revealed that they had been meticulously maintained by his valet Sydney Johnson.

Handkerchiefs mono-grammed with the imperial cypher of Edward VIII were unused, but those carrying the Prince of Wales cypher had seen heavy wear and were a fragile network of darning. Fifty handkerchiefs were sold as individual lots at the auction, raising $50,000.

The Duke of Windsor commissioned handmade shoes, favouring flamboyant co-respondent or spectator (two-tone) shoes for less formal occasions. Many were made for him by Peal & Co, a bootmaker established in the fourteenth-century, and some, daringly, had rubber soles, for though the duke liked to look good, he also favoured comfort. This style was associated with racy chaps and frowned on by polite society.

His father, George V, criticised him for wearing brogues, a country shoe, traditionally brown in colour, in the city – in line with the old adage: never wear brown in the town. The duke also stepped out in suede shoes, which were, at the time, regarded as a possible indicator of homosexuality.

Jane Eastoe

H.R.H. THE DUKE OF WINDSOR.

A cigarette card issued in 1937 for the coronation of George VI shows the former King some years previously. We cannot be sure the hand tinting reflects the true colours of this country outfit.

In by a short head

From our correspondent *June 18, 1999*

One lucky punter won £1,400 yesterday because the Queen wore a peach-coloured hat at Royal Ascot.

A Cardiff bookmaker took bets on the royal fashion stakes for Ladies' Day – and the mystery man won by placing £200 at 12-1. He won by a short head by deciding the Queen's hat would be peach.

The bookie, Paul Powell, said: "It was a fantastic selection. Peach was far from being the favourite."

Queen Elizabeth and Prince Phillip at Royal Ascot, June 17, 1999. The Queen wears Queen Mary's pearl and diamond brooch and pearl and diamond stud earrings and a three-string pearl necklace.

Above: Early in World War II Queen Elizabeth, aged 39, keeps things clean and stylish in this pale ensemble. It is a distinctly different look from the sugary pastels, flowers and feathers that became her uniform in her later role as Queen Mother.

Right: Princess Margaret makes quite the statement in this blue organza hat, royal in feel but distinctly 1960s in shape and proportion. It's worn with a blue floral dress, a two-string pearl necklace and a Cartier aquamarine and diamond brooch that was purchased by Queen Elizabeth the Queen Mother for £175 in 1947.

Left: Queen Elizabeth II steps out to a garden party in 1967 in sugar pink tailoring with grey accessories, Queen Mary's Dorset Bow Brooch and a floral flowerpot hat. Her Majesty's dresser, Bobo, had a stand-off with couturiers. To their chagrin she stated that while they were responsible for the clothes, she was in charge of the overall look. After years of gentle hints from the couturiers the Queen bowed to pressure and hats were specially designed alongside to suit.

Above: The Queen Mother blooms in an over-the-top hat laden with flowers and net, a style that provoked a thousand imitations.

Left: Queen Elizabeth II wears an uncharacteristically plain straw hat with a rounded upturned brim on a visit to Malta in November 1967. On a crisply tailored silk coat she wears a scattering of diamond brooches on her left shoulder.

Right: Then Duchess of Cornwall, now Queen Camilla, has always been fearless when it comes to hats, sporting a range of diverse shapes, from giant upturned brims to feathery and fanciful concoctions. She has been known to step out in a fascinator. Here she wears a cream, structural felt leaf hat to co-ordinate with her cream boucle coat and cream silk dress. This is a colour that always suits Queen Camilla.

Cornelia James

From our correspondent *December 18, 1999*

Cornelia James, glovemaker, died on December 10 aged 82. She was born on March 11, 1917.

Like many of those talented and determined middle Europeans displaced by Nazism, Cornelia James arrived in England with the baggage of a refugee but not the defensive attitude. Within days she and her younger sister, Susan, had made a list of the 1,000 largest companies in Britain and began a systematic and relentless barrage of calls to persuade them to agree to employ refugees from Austria – the more workplaces were allocated, the more refugees would be allowed in.

She spent the war doing occupational therapy for wounded soldiers, teaching them the complex skills of making gloves – which she had been studying in Vienna before the war.

After the war, when there was an acute shortage of clothing material for women, and all in drab colours, she realised that by producing brightly coloured gloves, using only small amounts of material, she could brighten the dullest outfit. Her bold designs rapidly brought her to the attentions of the royal couturiers Norman Hartnell and Hardy Amies, so that in 1947 she was asked to make the going-away gloves for the then Princess Elizabeth's family, as well as for department stores and couturiers in 45 countries.

The following spring she startled the fashion world by producing a range of leather gloves in 100 different colours and was christened "the Colour Queen of England" by *Vogue*. It was a sobriquet she loved. By the early 1950s her factory in Brighton was employing 500 people, and she was selling gloves to the British, Dutch, Swedish and Belgian royal families as well as to department stores and couturiers in 45 countries.

She was always a devout royalist, and her gloves are worn today not only by the Queen but by Queen Elizabeth the Queen Mother and the Princess Royal.

She once told her staff that Diana, Princess of Wales, had confessed that she would always be a good customer because she had a habit of biting her fingernails. In 1979 James was granted a Royal Warrant as Glove Manufacturer to the Queen. She was an active liveryman at the Worshipful Company of Glovers, and in 1989 she received the Freedom of the City. She was a tireless worker for charity all her life.

Glove-wearing is as much associated with the image of Queen Elizabeth II as hats and handbags. Born at a time when glove-wearing was de rigeur – nice young ladies would not consider leaving the house without a pair – Her Majesty may have been one of the last great glove-wearers. Norman Hartnell is reputed to have ordered a suitcase of gloves for the then Princess Elizabeth's trousseau. Her Majesty imbues daywear with a great deal of glamour in elbow-length gloves on a tour of Australia and New Zealand in 1953–4. The white lace dress is by Hardy Amies.

Left: Queen Elizabeth's gloves were made by Cornelia James, who started making them for her in the 1940s and continued until Her Majesty's death. Here, on tour of Australia in 1954, Her Majesty wears a pair of mid-arm gloves in white to match her other accessories. Glove-wearing, as well as being polite, served to protect Her Majesty when shaking hands with so many people. Unusually she is carrying her handbag on her right arm, generally she carries it on her left. Over the course of her long reign switching her bag from left to right arm is said to be a signal to her Ladies-in-Waiting that she may need assistance in moving on.

H.R.H. PRINCESS MARGARET.   721

Above: Princess Margaret wears a pair of over-the-elbow gloves in 1952 to add to the glamorous effect of her Dior dress. Evening gloves make a wonderful foil for good jewellery and they are adjusted in fit to suit the individual. Cornelia James, a refugee from Vienna after Austria was invaded in 1938, started to make gloves as a living and created a brightly coloured leather range. There was little money for clothing, which was rationed, but women could buy accessories to update their look. She rapidly became known as the person to go to for good gloves and the company still supplies many members of the royal family, as well stars of the film and music industries.

Guards take aim at bearskins

By Michael Evans, Defence Editor

May 10, 2005

Trials have begun to test a potential breakthrough in artificial fur that may replace the bearskin ceremonial caps worn for nearly two centuries by the Foot Guard regiments.

The alternative to the glossy black bear fur of the Guards' imposing ceremonial caps is being tested by the textiles agency for the services. Samples are also being examined by the Guards. The British Army has been trying for ten years to find an alternative to the bearskin fur because of rising complaints from animal welfare pressure groups, who have accused the Guards of being party to the slaughter of thousands of bears every year in Canada.

The Household Division has countered the animal rights case with the defence that none of the bears culled has been killed because of an order for bearskins from the Army.

A spokesman for the Household Division, which comprises the Grenadier Guards, Coldstream Guards, Scots Guards, Irish Guards and Welsh Guards, said: "Twenty thousand black bears have to be culled in North America each year, from which we buy fewer than 100 pelts a year for the Guards' bearskin caps."

Prince Harry, who has just started his first term at the Royal Military Academy Sandhurst, could be among those to wear bearskins with artificial fur if he joins the Welsh Guards.

This was his original choice, although he is now believed to be leaning more towards the Blues and Royals or the Life Guards of the Household Cavalry.

One of the most vociferous animal rights organisations that has been campaigning against the Household Division's historic use of real black bear fur is now planning to demonstrate against the Queen when she goes on an official visit to Canada on a week today.

A member of the People for the Ethical Treatment of Animals (PETA) is proposing to dress as a bear and stalk the Queen during her ten-day tour. Andrew Butler, the campaign co-ordinator for PETA, said: "It is outrageous that bears continue to be killed in Canada for a ceremonial hat in Britain."

The Household Division said that this argument was totally wrong and that bear pelts were made available only because of the annual cull that had to be carried out to keep bear numbers under control.

Her Majesty is most definitely amused as she walks past her husband, in a bearskin, at Buckingham Palace in 2005. The Duke of Edinburgh was Honorary Colonel of the Grenadier Guards. Technically referred to as a fur cap, the bearskin was introduced sometime in 1768, but its use for anything other than ceremonial occasions was discontinued in the nineteenth-century; keeping the headwear in good condition was too problematic. They were last worn in battle during the Crimean War. The fur cap is associated with the British Foot Guard regiments and is worn by the Grenadier Guards, Coldstream Guards, Scots Guards, Irish Guards, and Welsh Guards as part of their dress uniform, as well as officers of the Fusilier Regiments, the Royal Scots Dragoon Guards and the Honorary Artillery Company.

A Ministry of Defence spokesman said: "Bears are not shot for their fur. Bearskin is used from animals shot by Canadian Rangers or licensed hunters." However, the results of trials of an artificial fur are being awaited to see if industry has finally come up with a solution.

The Household Division spokesman said: "None of the previous tests on artificial fur has proved any good. Either the artificial fur soaked up water, or it became discoloured or, in some cases, when there was static in the air, the hair stood on end."

Unlike busbies, worn by the King's Troop Royal Horse Artillery and some military bands, which are pillbox-shaped and used to consist of tight beaver hair, the tall bearskin caps worn by the Guards regiments have long and luxurious bear fur, and all attempts to re-create the same effect without damaging consequences have failed.

Fur for busbies has been artificial for some years without suffering the problems of waterlogging, discolouration and "hair-raising". If the latest fur technology solves the problem, replacing the bearskin fur would take place as caps come in for refurbishment. Mr Butler said: "Our bear [in Canada] will follow the Queen to demand an immediate ceasefire for the bears while the modern synthetic bearskins are being tested."

Above and right: The standard bearskin measures 11 inches (28cms) at the front and 16 inches (41cms) at the rear. It weighs in at an impressive 1.5 pounds (0.68kg), and it gets heavier when wet. The height of the cap varies slightly from regiment to regiment and can vary according to rank. A bamboo cage supports the structure of the cap and the pelt or fabric (depending on age) can be shampooed and conditioned by its owner to keep it looking in tip-top condition. Fur caps are also sent for re-conditioning by specialists at intervals. An adjustable leather skullcap and chin strap that sits below the lips ensure a snug fit.

Where Meghan buys her clothes from (it matters)

By Hattie Crisell   *January 24, 2018*

There aren't many well-kept secrets in the fashion industry. In general it's a world in which if on Monday you entrust a friend with a juicy tale, by Tuesday an unknown assistant will be holding court at a magazine shoot, relaying it to a stylist, a photographer, an editor, two celebrities and the intern who just came back from the coffee run.

When it comes to the business of dressing a royal, however, mouths snap closed like one of the Queen's Launer handbags. And when the individual in question is a glamorous American princess-to-be, who gathers more rapt followers by the hour, things get especially fraught.

You may be one of those who are infuriated by how much attention the press gives to Meghan Markle's wardrobe – but forgive me for adding to the noise because

I find that the closer I delve into the circus the more intriguing it becomes. It's not only hacks giving Markle's clothing heavy scrutiny, nor is it only her legions of fans, who run Twitter accounts with such names as @meghanm-daily, @whatmeghanwore and @madaboutmeghan. Somewhere behind the gates of Kensington Palace Markle's wardrobe has become a project, every detail researched carefully for the perfect blend of diplomacy and elegance.

If you're sceptical that finding a few outfits in which Markle can wave at crowds and deliver twinkly smiles to children could possibly be a complicated job, just consider some of her recent appearances. On Thursday she made her first official visit to Wales, delivering a PR boost for British brands in a coat by Stella McCartney and velvet boots by Tabitha

Simmons. Her jeans, more importantly, were by Hiut Denim. Never heard of it? That's the point.

Her clothes are also a way of discreetly sketching out the kind of royal she plans to be. Last week she carried a green Mini Venice bag by another little-known label called DeMellier, which has its own charitable initiative: for every bag sold, the brand pays for a set of vaccines and life-saving treatments for a child in the developing world. For a woman entering into a public life it was a much cleverer move than a designer It bag.

Markle has made only a handful of public appearances since the engagement, but the examples of considered styling continue. Her Marks & Spencer jumper was the right relatable choice for a visit to Repreze 107.3 FM in Brixton, south London,

Meghan Markle created a retail frenzy when she carried this Strathberry midi tote in December 2017, seen here as the Duchess of Sussex on a later visit to Dublin, Ireland in July 2018.

two weeks ago. The rest of it seems to be about giving airtime to companies that absolutely are not household names: the bag she carried on a trip to Nottingham in December came from small luxury Scottish brand Strathberry, who cheerfully told me they had sold out within minutes.

The same goes for DeMellier. Mireia Llusia-Lindh, the founder and creative director, only worked out what was happening via Twitter, after noticing an enormous increase in traffic to the brand's site. "Suddenly we saw it: Meghan Markle is wearing one of our bags," she tells me. "We were like, 'Oh my God, oh my God!'" When Llusia-Lindh looked at orders, she could see the bag had been ordered to a Kensington postcode a few days earlier. "It is fantastic for a smaller up-and-coming British brand like us."

Not even on the fashion desk of *The Times* had everyone heard of some of these niche labels, so what are the chances that they were familiar to Markle – an American actress who was based in the UK for about five minutes? Nil, I suspect. She's getting help.

My calls and emails to those labels, in an attempt to work out how the process works, are met with varying degrees of panic. No one seems to know what they are allowed to reveal.

Marks & Spencer does confirm that someone at Kensington Palace bought Markle's jumper and told the store when she would be wearing it.

Several PRs stall for time. One says: "We've been told not to say anything," then refuses to explain whether this is a directive from the top or just an internal policy. Kensington Palace will say nothing except that "members of the royal family do not accept gifts, so clothes are paid for." Presumably that stretches to future members too.

Meghan Markle opts to wear her Strathberry East/West Midi bag across the body on a visit to Edinburgh in February, 2018. This would be a radical move for a royal, but at this point Meghan was still a mere Miss until her wedding in May 2018. A feature of the brand is the Strathberry bar fastening. If you didn't know it was a visit to Scotland the tartan coat confirms as much. One wonders who suggested to a doubtless mystified Meghan that the wearing of a tartan anything is practically compulsory for a royal visit to Scotland.

ACKNOWLEDGEMENTS

It would feel churlish not to begin without expressing my gratitude to the royal family, past and present for working so hard to look fabulous when heading out and about. To be exposed to such constant public scrutiny and criticism would break most of us. I admire their commitment and effort and their ongoing support of British fashion; a much maligned industry which generates income and employment for thousands upon thousands of people and which supports the livelihoods of countless designers, craftspeople, and artisans as well as manufacturers and retailers. I salute you.

At HarperCollins I must thank my editor Harley Griffiths and the editorial project manager, Evangeline Sellers, who have both supported me through the process of producing this book. Their patience, consideration, commitment and professionalism has been more precious than rubies. Thanks must also go to *The Times* Fashion Director Anna Murphy for so kindly agreeing to write the foreword.

I must also thank the superb photographer and artist Harry Cory Wright, who graciously gave us permission to reproduce some of his photographs. The man is a genius.

At News UK Archives I must thank Chris Ball and Michael-John Jennings for their support in navigating The Times archive and for their incredible research skills.

On the domestic front I salute and thank my husband, Eric Musgrave. Quite apart from his tireless devotion to dressing well, his brain, which I shamelessly picked, is simply stuffed with information about menswear, tailoring, uniforms and textiles. He was of immense practical help and support in the researching and writing of this book. Couldn't have managed it without you darling.

Final thanks must go to Shannon Denson without whose understanding I would never have managed this project.

PICTURE CREDITS

p.249: Max Mumby / Indigo / Getty Images
p.250: Harry Cory Wright
p.251: PA Images / Alamy Stock Photo
p.252–253: PA Images / Alamy Stock Photo
p.256: Harry Cory Wright
p.257: Harry Cory Wright
p.259: Universal Art Archive / Alamy Stock Photo
p.260: Popperfoto / Getty Images
p.261: Popperfoto / Getty Images
p.263: Bethany Clarke / Stringer
p.265: W. and D. Downey / Stringer
p.266: SuperStock / Alamy Stock Photo
p.267: Chronicle / Alamy Stock Photo
p.269: PA Images / Alamy Stock Photo
p.270: Hulton Archive / Stringer
p.273: The Print Collector / Alamy Stock Photo
p.275: Tim Graham / Getty Images
p.276: Sueddeutsche Zeitung Photo / Alamy Stock Photo
p.277: Ray Bellisario/Popperfoto / Contributor
p.278: PA Images / Alamy Stock Photo
p.279: Keystone Press / Alamy Stock Photo
p.280: Fox Photos / Stringer
p.281: Max Mumby / Indigo / Getty Images
p.282: Alpha Historica / Alamy Stock Photo
p.284: Popperfoto / Getty Images
p.285: Chronicle / Alamy Stock Photo
p.287: Anwar Hussein / Getty Images
p.288: The Times / News Licensing
p.289: The Times / News Licensing
p.291: Matt Crossick / Alamy Stock Photo
p.293: newsphoto / Alamy Stock Photo
p.294–295: Independent / Alamy Stock Photo
Back cover: Tim Graham / Getty Images

Photo captions

Front cover image: A 19-year-old Princess Margaret in a post-war photograph by Cecil Beaton, taken in 1949.

p.4: Norman Hartnell submitted nine sketches for Queen Elizabeth II to choose the design for her Coronation dress. His eighth sketch was selected, but it was proposed that the embroidery be in colour rather than all silver. Her Majesty also requested that the Welsh emblem and the emblems of the Commonwealth countries be added to the motifs on the dress.

p.6–7: Diana, Princess of Wales, and Prince William at the Guard's Polo Club in May, 1988.

The princess wears jeans, a blazer, possibly by Turnbull & Asser, a British Lung Foundation sweatshirt and a pair of cowboy boots.

p.12–13: The Duchess of Windsor was photographed in this famous off-white silk "Lobster dress" by Schiaparelli which was revealed to the public in the designer's 1937 summer/fall collection. The dress features a large red lobster on the front and sprigs of parsley, the original design for this was painted by Salvador Dali who saw lobsters as a symbol of sexuality. Cecil Beaton photographed her in items from her trousseau shortly before her wedding to the former King Edward VIII in June 1937.

p.18–19: Prince George and Princess Mary on their wedding day in 1893. They had ten bridesmaids, two were the bridegroom's sisters, Princess Victoria and Princess Maud of Wales.

p.34–35: Prince Albert's wedding to Elizabeth Bowes-Lyon was seen as a modern step for although Elizabeth was the daughter of a peer, she was not royal by blood. Traditionally the royal family had only married other royals, though there are a few notable exceptions in history, not least Henry VIII.

p.58–59: The new Duke of Windsor, shortly after his abdication from the British throne, is reunited with Wallis Simpson at the Château de Candé in France, May 1937. They make a crisp and pristine pair.

p.92–93: Emulating Queen Victoria, HM Queen Elizabeth II chose six Maids of Honour to take care of her train at her coronation on June 2, 1953. Lady Moyra Hamilton, Lady Anne Coke, Lady Rosemary Spencer-Churchill, Lady Mary Baillie-Hamilton, Lady Jane Heathcote-Drummond-Willoughby and Lady Jane Vane-Tempest-Stewart, who were aged between 19 and 23, wore embroidered dresses designed by Norman Hartnell, who also created the Queen's gown. Next to the Queen is her aunt, Princess Marina.

p.124–125: King Charles III wore the heavyweight St Edward's Crown for the ceremony, changing to the lighter Imperial Crown to depart. This contains the Black Prince's ruby, the Stuart sapphire and the Cullinan II diamond. In the interests of sustainability and efficiency Queen Camilla did not commission a new crown for her coronation. Instead she utilised Queen Mary's Crown. Under her robes she wore a white dress, designed by Bruce Oldfield, with silver and gold embroidery.

p.130–131: Queen Elizabeth and the Duke of Windsor attend the annual Garter ceremony in Windsor, June 1999. The Sovereign's mantle has the longest train which has to be carried by page boys.

p.132–133: Queen Elizabeth II comes face to face with another icon when she meets Marilyn Monroe at the Royal Film Performance of *The Battle of the River Plate*, October 1956. It was very rare for the queen to wear black, but in this instance she was advised by her couturier Norman Hartnell to go for a subtle approach and let her magnificent jewellery stand out to best advantage. Monroe was in England filming *The Prince and the Showgirl*, her dress did not meet the standards of royal protocol which requested that nothing too revealing was worn. Both women were aged 30 at the time, Monroe was born just two months after the queen.

p.154–155: A selection of Queen Elizabeth II's sorbet coloured evening dresses designed by Norman Hartnell in the 1950s. All were exhibited at the *Fashioning a Reign* Exhibition at Windsor Castle in 2016. Each one is pin pricked with the tell-tale marks left by brooches and orders.

p.172–173: Princess Anne looks more stylish in jeans, black polo-neck, and cap than ever she does dressed up to the nines. Here, at Eridgepark in 1971, the 21-year-old princess teases fellow equestrian Richard Meade.

p.176–177: A regular visitor to the spa town of Bad Homburg, in Hesse, Germany, Bertie, Prince of Wales, popularised the smart hat that carries the town's name. Here, in 1882, he is accompanied by a sextet of well-dressed cronies.

p.188–189: Prescription country dressing from the Duke and Duchess of York on honeymoon in 1923. A symphony of beige and brown, but it is the hats that really signal off duty.

p.194–195: Prince Philip Duke of Edinburgh and Princess Anne enjoy some down time in 1964. The 14-year-old princess looks refreshingly good with short hair, a cap and a simple shirt.

p.212–213: On a Royal tour of India in 1961 Queen Elizabeth II wears a lavender organza duster coat and matching dress with a perfectly toning hat, naturally plus pearls, gloves and handbag. On her shoulder is the magnificent Duchess of Teck's Corsage Brooch.

p.252–253: Princess Margaret purchased the Poltimore Tiara at an auction in 1959 for £5,500. She wore it at her wedding and to many other formal occasions and was even photographed wearing it in the bath by her husband, Lord Snowdon. It can also transform into a necklace or 11 different brooches. After her death in 2002 the family sold it at auction for £926,400, its whereabouts are unknown.

p.294–295: Sparkling in the Diamond Diadem, Queen Elizabeth II leaves the Palace of Westminster after the State Opening of Parliament in November, 2006.